Something About Suffering:

What My Child's Death Taught Me About God's Love

TAYLOR KEEFER

Something About Suffering:
What My Child's Death Taught Me About God's Love

Copyright © 2023 by Taylor Keefer

Cover design © 2023 Taylor Keefer

taylorelizabethkeefer@gmail.com
taylorelizabethkeefer.com

Contents

Acknowledgment iv

Preface v

Chapter 1: What Lies Ahead 1

Chapter 2: Shattered Chandeliers 8

Chapter 3: Trusting the One Who Takes 25

Chapter 4: Things That May Never Come 38

Chapter 5: Where They Leave You 55

Chapter 6: The Way of Paradoxes 74

Chapter 7: Blessings Still Grow on the Valley Floor 88

Chapter 8: Thy Will Be Done 103

Chapter 9: Healing Waits For You 114

Chapter 10: Tree of Life 127

Chapter 11: All the Parts Suffer With It 144

Chapter 12: When You Must Bury 153

To Jude, From Mom 161

To Jude, From Dad 164

Acknowledgment

Most importantly, I dedicate this work to God, the giver of all good things. May his guiding Spirit empower my words to honor Jude, bring glory to his name, and provide comfort to many.

Secondly, this labor of love is dedicated to my precious firstborn, Jude. It is an honor to carry this grief, knowing it is the price I paid for the privilege of knowing and loving you. Oh, what I would have done to give you more time, little one. Until we meet again.

Lastly, I want to acknowledge my husband, Jack. Thank you for walking with me through the darkest of all valleys. You carried me when I could no longer stand, and for that, you have my eternal admiration.

Preface

I will begin by telling you what this book is not. It is not a broom intended to sweep up the broken fragments of your life. It is not a translator that can interpret meaning for you. It is not a map to guide you to the next destination. The story of my son's life is not a simple one. It was a mess of tragedy and blessing, both of which I will be teasing apart between these pages. I do not consider myself a writer of extraordinary ability, but a human with a heart that bleeds alongside yours.

I would like to share these gifts with you, both of darkness and of light, without judgment or dismissal of either one. As uncomfortable as it may be to acknowledge both, it's important to notice the knife that cuts the deepest wounds still cannot reach the depths of our love.

For those who may have never experienced child loss, I want you to know that grief is a shared human experience. Though you may be separated from my specific circumstances, please allow me to sit in the same space as you, united by the suffering and sorrow we all experience to varying degrees.

Similarly, I hope to allow this story to be told in honor of those who have undoubtedly walked through flames that have burned at a greater intensity than mine. May we hold grace for each other and acknowledge the lives lived and the lives lost.

I do not suppose that I will soften your suffering or make it purposeful, only that I might suggest there exists hope that there is someone who one day will.

1

What Lies Ahead

"Beloved, do not be surprised at the fiery trial when it comes upon you to test you, as though something strange were happening to you."
- 1 Peter 4:12 (ESV)

There's a storm out there, you know.

Its crimson skies swirl counterclockwise with winds exceeding 400 miles per hour. At 10,000 miles across, this hurricane is large enough to swallow the entire Earth.

It's known as the Great Red Spot on the planet Jupiter and it's been raging on for the last several hundred years. As you commute to work, lay your child down to sleep, or curl up on your living room couch, the Great Red Spot roars out just beyond our blue skies. Its high pressures and turbulent winds are strong enough to tear you to pieces.

Astronomers have diligently monitored this violent storm since the 1800s, so we have come to learn much about it. What we can't seem to figure out is exactly why this vortex has been so persistent, where it's getting its energy from, and what chemical compounds are creating its glowing, fiery hue. It's as mysterious as it is powerful.

Have you ever stopped to thank your lucky stars that you do not live on a planet that creates persistent, hostile, 400-year-long hurricanes? Of course you haven't, because we've got our own set of natural disasters to deal with. They might pale in comparison to the Great Red Spot, but they remain tragedies nonetheless. When you are steering a battered boat braving 50 foot waves while the sea brutally pounds against your legs, you are not mindfully jotting down in your gratitude journal that at least the waves are not 100 feet.

The storms of this world take shape in many terrifying ways, puncturing our hearts with fear as we frantically seek shelter. Some tear away your home, chewing through family photo albums and ripping out the beloved tree your dad tied a swing to when you were six years old. Some are catastrophic enough that you swear you'll never take anything for granted again. But you'll forget. Some summon charcoal clouds, draping a darkness of desolation and disorientation over you. You'll need to learn to tolerate that disorientation because all anyone can offer you are their best hopes, coated with the glossy paint of momentary clarity, so that they might resemble answers upon first glance. Look again. Some leave us no other option than to accept our fate. And, depending on what you've gone through up until that point, death might be but a spider on your wall that you keep your eye on but don't mind much. There are things worse than death.

Nevertheless, I am certain of one thing: a storm is approaching. It's coming right for you. You may be reminded to remain on high alert when you discover the disaster that has destroyed your friend's life, or a family member's. Even so, it will remain an intellectual abstract — something that happened to other people. It is human nature to underestimate the destructive power of mother nature. We all get fooled by the monotony of life, the glassy waters, the warmth of the tea in our hands. It only takes moments for the rogue wave to appear. By the time tsunamis become visible on the shoreline, it is already too late.

I admit, you may not suffer extreme tragedy. It might not be a disease that is spreading or a loved one buried. But it might be an unexpected diagnosis. It might be a debilitating addiction. It might be a child born with permanent disabilities. It might be the crushing injustice that fuels the suffering of those around you. It might be a closed door you always expected to walk through. It might be something lost that can never be found.

This year, I experienced my very own Great Red Spot. It was a vortex big enough to swallow the entire Earth. It was mighty and mysterious. It was agonizing and alien. It was holy and hallowed. It was a storm others gazed at from their telescopes, eyes wide, silently muttering gratitude that they did not live on such a wretched planet. For me, it was the death of my firstborn son, Jude.

Jude always showed himself to be an active and free-spirited baby while he was still protected in my womb. He jumped between the hands of every midwife who checked on him, like he was happy to sense them again. It was often a struggle just to check his heartbeat because he would kick at the fetal doppler. Even in his final months, despite the challenges he faced (or perhaps because of them), he was enraptured by life. He would grasp my face between his two chubby hands and flash me his two top teeth with a radiant smile. Our home was filled with his laughter, bubble baths, and a floor strewn with books. Nothing quite entertained him like a good book, as long as you helped him turn the pages. Despite his tremendous child-like ability to be fully present, books showed that even he, like all of us, was perpetually intrigued by what came next.

Allow me to kill the suspense. While I might not know what awaits you next or what may have already happened in a previous chapter, I know that to exist is to suffer. From the moment of our birth, death ensnared us, and pain cradled us in its arms, filling our lungs with cries before we ever had a chance to feel the warmth of our mother's skin against ours.

This suffering is a sure thing. These storms will surely come, and they should not be met with cheerful dismissal. Some storms do not spare lives, while others leave you begging for death. Tragedies cannot be tied with a bow, nor can they be crafted into comeback stories ringing platitudes about how everything happens for a reason.

Do you know what it's like to hold a dead child in your arms?

I do.

There is nothing that would stop me from making it not so. No amount of positive change his death may have sparked, whether parents now love their children more profoundly or medical professionals have had their faith rekindled, can ever justify his death. Similarly, there is no introspective personal growth earnest enough to condone this loss. To do so would contradict the fundamental nature of the parent-child relationship, as my life should be for his benefit, not the other way around.

When it's your child's life, there is no rationale that satisfies. Love marches into our lives with its demands of luxury suites and ocean views. It wants to have its cake and eat it too. It puts on the kid's oxygen mask before its own. It's entirely irrational and helplessly unreasonable.

Pain is like that too.

There's nothing that will prompt you to talk to (or scream at) God quite like suffering through the storm. There is no hard-earned belief in self-reliance strong enough to withstand those winds.

The night before the crucifixion of Jesus Christ, the Bible tells us even Jesus desperately prayed to the Father to spare him. Likewise, our human, finite hearts cry out to the God of the universe that there must be another way. We see the wave barreling toward us and beg for God to intervene instead of allowing it to violently crash upon us, plunging our shattered bodies against the ocean floor.

If you have made it this far, allow me to present to you my humble proposition that God has a relationship with suffering. In fact, I have married the two in my mind. When I spent month after month in the pediatric intensive care unit with my son, it did not feel like an unfortunate accident that occurred while God had his hands tied, shrugging sheepishly in the shadow of evil he could not overpower. It felt purposeful. That is not to say God is some sadistic creature with my bleeding body hanging from his fangs — although I would be lying if I said I didn't sometimes feel that way — but God is not entirely separate from the suffering you and I experience. He is not controlled by it; instead, he dwells in it. He uses it. There's something about suffering that goes beyond our understanding, something he perceives that we do not. He is the voice on the other side, urging us to hold on, promising the darkness does not endure forever. Somehow, in some way, he assures us that all of this will ultimately be worthwhile.

Consider the pain of birth. It's a bloody, screaming, white-knuckling, and leg-buckling mess. It's a pain you can't bear to breathe through, let alone speak through — unless, of course, it's for profanity or the proclamation that you truly cannot do this. But you don't really have a choice. That's quite similar to the pain of death. In this life, we get to experience the "worthwhile" aftermath of labor pains. We receive a miracle into our arms that redeems it all, oxytocin coursing through our veins. It's the most dramatic perspective shift a human can experience, powerful enough to convince some to willingly undergo the anguish once more.

Is it reasonable to assume death could be the same way?

Perhaps, we're simply still in the season of contractions, unable to believe we can withstand this, unable to imagine a reward large enough to alleviate this pain. If we could only see what has been hidden for a short time, we might look back on our seasons of suffering as a burden worth bearing over and over again.

God sometimes uses or allows for the disorder and violence in our world for his purposes. In the same way forests require wildfires to increase fertility and promote a greater biodiversity to thrive, the biblical narrative cycles through a profound pattern of decreation and new creation, enabling life to emerge from the ashes. Some of this destruction is incidental, but much of it illustrates God's choice to weave together a redemptive story for humans who continually inflict pain upon one another. We see time and again that God's ultimate will for us all is to have life abundantly, not to succumb to death. Genesis 50:20 reads:

"You intended to harm me, but God intended it for good to accomplish what is now being done, the saving of many lives."

The God who both gives and takes away allowed Jude to take his last breath in my arms, the day after his first birthday — and I know this is a reality that unsettles many. We like to interpret tragedies through the lens of blame, either placing blame on a God who permits such terrible things or on the devil, whom we imagine has God bound and gagged in some basement, yet still granting him free rein to sow chaos into our lives. Or we'd like to throw up our hands in defeat and say we live in a chaotic world where meaningless pain happens, which I believe is somewhat true. I don't have answers for you about the nature of suffering, and I'm not convinced we would fully comprehend them even if we did. It's not about getting the answers, because you will rarely have them. It's about embracing the questions. It's about paddling into those dark and chaotic waves, knowing that's where truth lies, resisting the urge to return to the familiar shoreline. Even when the unanswered questions become too heavy, spilling from your pockets and slipping off your shoulders, God will continue to teach, speak, listen, and provide for your needs according to his will.

And so, though I don't have answers, I have a few thoughts to share with you. I trust that you will meet with me here in between the pages. My storm left me devastated, but there exists a hidden place in my heart where the floodwaters nurtured a garden. It's a sanctuary where a babbling brook of tears flows, and wildflowers lean toward the echoes of Jude's laughter lingering in the golden glow of the sun. If you take my hand, I will lead you along the trail and dig my knuckles into the damp soil. I will show you what I have buried there.

2

Shattered Chandeliers

"Jesus replied, 'You do not realize now what I am doing, but later you will understand.'"
- John 13:7 (NIV)

Some say Jude was born with "angel numbers." He came into this world at 5:55 a.m. on 5/22/22, a date that also marked my mother's 50th birthday. He spent 220 days in the hospital, which equates to 7 months (5+2). These little details always served as a poignant reminder to my husband, Jack, and me that, amidst a series of statistical anomalies, everything about Jude appeared remarkably precise.

If ever there was a moment when we felt profoundly blessed by God, it was when we gazed upon our firstborn. Jack and I both have dark features, so we were pleasantly surprised when we were greeted by our blonde-haired, blue-eyed boy. I loved that Jude looked so different from us; it emphasized the feeling that he was not entirely of us but rather an angel bestowed upon us for a brief, precious time.

Postpartum life was slow and all of Jude's check-ups followed a predictable and uneventful routine. Though his healthy life could have been received as a miraculous display of God's grace, I'll admit that it was simply in line with my expectations. We had received excellent prenatal care, I diligently took all my vitamins, maintained a balanced diet, exercised regularly, became pregnant at a young and healthy age, and spent month after month covering my baby in prayer. I merely expected a rich harvest to grow from good soil.

After a little over a week of heavenly newborn snuggles and green flags from pediatrician appointments, lactation consultations, and many postnatal midwife visits, Jack and I decided to take Jude on his first outing at 11 days old. Our friends met up on Thursday nights for a Bible study, and on June 2, 2022, they were having their last get together before their summer hiatus. It seemed like a perfect opportunity for everyone to meet 11-day-old Jude. I was only planning on stopping by for a few minutes to socialize and drop off some dessert before heading back home.

Jude was sleepy that day, but it was nothing out of the ordinary for a newborn. We took his temperature in the morning because it was a warm day, but he showed no signs of fever. When we arrived at our friend's house that evening, Jude was fussing a lot, so I held him in a carrier while I nursed him. He was still irritable, but eventually it seemed like he had fallen asleep. After a few minutes of chatting with our friends, I figured it was a good time for everyone to see Jude since he had been fast asleep for a while. My heart stopped when I pulled his head out of my carrier. His head dropped heavily. His skin was pale. I had never seen, much less held, a dead body before.

I did not have a pit in my stomach, but a black hole, forming in mere seconds after my soul had collapsed in on itself. In shock, my mind raced to provide me with alternative hypotheses. Perhaps, it was just the lighting. My husband and I ran out of the house and to our car where I immediately ripped the carrier off my shoulders and threw it across the backseat. I pulled Jude onto my lap, removing him from his swaddle. His limbs flopped to the side of his body. His eyes were closed and his mouth hung open lifelessly. His skin was already cold, his complexion gray, and he held no pulse. The realization he was indeed dead was instantaneous. The moment I had thought he had fallen asleep nearly 15 minutes ago was likely the moment his heart had stopped beating. My son had died in my arms, and I hadn't even noticed.

I began hyperventilating as Jack called 911 while peeling out of the neighborhood. We would have an ambulance meet us if they could, but we weren't wasting any more time. It felt as if there was a giant digital clock over our heads, our car walls collapsing in more and more with each passing second. It takes everything I've got to forgive myself for how paralyzed I was in that moment. If it hadn't been for Jack, I have no idea what I would have done. The fear coiled itself around my body like a snake, suffocating me and rendering my lungs incapable of expanding, my mouth from speaking, my arms from moving. As Jack sped through red lights, blaring the horn, he managed to get us to the nearest emergency room just two minutes away, even before 911 could dispatch help.

It's tragic moments like this that people often use as evidence that life can spin out of control in an instant, leaving your world shattered and the life you knew forever altered. In a way, that's undeniably true. As I sprinted my baby's corpse through those emergency room doors, pleading for help, the last thing I felt was any sense of control. Yet, the truth remains that each of us possess some measure of control, granted by God, although it is inherently limited. It's essentially risk management. You can't control every aspect of your life all the time.

You can diligently apply sunscreen and still receive a skin cancer diagnosis, maintain an impeccable track record and still have a supervisor deem your work unsatisfactory, take all of your prenatal vitamins and still experience a miscarriage, remain faithful and still face infidelity, or invest everything into a business that still fails. Control is a common method our brains use to process information. When something positive happens for someone, it's often attributed to their virtuous actions. Conversely, if misfortune falls, it's tempting to believe they must have made some error along the way. This phenomenon that good things happen to good people is known as the just-world theory, and it serves as a protective mechanism. It shields people from confronting the harsh reality that their own storms may also be on the horizon, and there might not always be a way to prevent them.

The truth is, we do wield a degree of power, but we are far from omnipotent. Life typically adheres to general principles, but exceptions abound. Sometimes people fall in between the cracks of the general rule of thumb, becoming outliers. These are the unfortunate ones we pity but secretly believe we could never become. For me and my husband, unfortunately, this would be the beginning of a long journey of parenthood that was not following standard procedure. "When Your Baby Dies in Your Arms" wasn't a chapter I remembered reading in any baby book.

Medical professionals scattered into organized chaos the moment we ran through those doors and they caught a glimpse of Jude's gray arm dangling helplessly out of his swaddle. With limited power over the situation, the medical staff encircled Jude. As he was placed on the nearest hospital bed, the emergency response reminded me of the speed at which a bullet leaves a gun — too fast to process. The staff gathered in the doorway while a trembling scribe attempted to document the proceedings. At the time, I possessed no comprehension of the medical protocols applicable in such an emergency.

I miss that about myself — the innocence and naivety

that rendered me incapable of understanding the tragedy transpiring before me, unable to explain the efforts being undertaken to save him. However, having spent countless hours in an ICU setting since that fateful day, I can now fill the gaps for you with a little more clarity.

To monitor Jude's vital signs, they connected him to a pulse oximeter and placed ECG wires to his chest, commonly referred to as "leads." These leads come in black, white, and red, and to remember their placement, they used the mnemonic "white over right, smoke over fire." The white electrode is placed on the patient's right side of the chest, the black is placed on the patient's left side, and the red is placed beneath the white on the left side of the abdomen. In Jude's case, these vital signs were futile because he was not in ventricular fibrillation, tachycardia, or bradycardia as is often seen in most cardiac arrest cases. Jude arrived at the emergency room in asystole, which meant he was clinically dead. He had no heartbeat. The American College of Emergency Physicians and National Association of Emergency Medical Services Physicians both provide written protocols that allow for termination of resuscitation efforts for a select group of patients in which further measures would be considered futile. Jude had fallen into this category. In every medical sense, he was labeled hopeless.

Typically, defibrillators would be used to stop the chaotic rhythm of the heart so that it can return to its natural beating rhythm, but there is no shock-able rhythm when the heart's electrical system has shut down entirely. Defibrillators can be life-saving in the event of a heart that has stopped pumping blood, but not for one that has stopped beating. In such rare cases, medical professionals have very limited options. This was not a life they could save, but a life they had to bring back from death.

They initiated CPR, and an intraosseous (IO)

line was inserted into Jude's 11-day-old shin. An IO is a means of rapidly administering emergency medication like epinephrine. It involves drilling into the bone so the medication can travel through the marrow, the pressure of which is excruciating if the patient were to be conscious. To provide ventilation, Jude was immediately intubated, with a tube inserted into his throat and down into the windpipe to supply oxygen to his lungs.

Amidst these frantic efforts to bring Jude back to life, all of which I struggled to comprehend, it's hard to say how much time passed in that moment — but my mind found ways to keep track. I tracked it by the number of times they announced they couldn't find a pulse. I tracked it by noticing when a nurse rolled over a chair for me because I had been standing too long. I tracked it by following the growing column of numbers on the whiteboard in front of me, marking the times when each drug was administered. If you're one of the unlucky ones, you can track it by the way the energy in the room settles, much like the silence that follows a firework bursting in the sky, with light dispersing into the night. The dark black cloud of death hovering over the room descended onto our heads, over our eyes, enveloping our bodies and suffocating the chaos from the room.

Less movements being made.

Fewer drugs being administered.

I tracked it by seeing the medical staff on either side of my baby exchange prolonged glances as the room grew quieter. I tracked it when, in the corner of my eye, I caught a glimpse of a nurse walking over to me, wrapping her arm around my shoulders. I turned to look at her, and she gazed past me, directly at Jude, her eyes reflecting the devastating scene. She absorbed the situation with much more medical comprehension and awareness than I had the capacity for. When she finished reading the equation, the solution clearly written before her, she translated it for me by looking back into my eyes, hers wet with tears. She placed a gentle hand on my shoulder and, with a shaky voice, managed to utter one painful sentence:

"I'm *so sorry.*"

You would think I would be on the floor praying, but I wasn't. I stood in the corner, keeping my distance, clinging tightly to Jude's swaddle — the very swaddle I had carefully wrapped him in before putting him to bed. This particular swaddle had earned its place on my baby registry after meticulous consideration of its quality, made from nontoxic, organic cotton. It was the swaddle I softly folded and placed in our closet, nine months pregnant, eagerly awaiting Jude's arrival. I clung to it like I was clinging to the life that existed just an hour ago. I clung to it like the hope for our lives to resume as it always had. I clung to it because I couldn't bear to enter into this storm that consumed everything in front of me. The swaddle remained as the last tangible relic of a life that had irrevocably vanished. I was almost unwilling to drop it, to let go of what once was to accept what will now be — as if I had a choice. As if life waits for our permission.

The only prayer that my mind could muster was distilled into a single word, echoing ceaselessly through my thoughts: "Please." I had involuntarily linked arms with every parent who has walked this Earth and has faced the threat of their child dying in front of them, whether due to sickness or crime or tragedy. We are the ones who kneel in pools of blood, who watch our loved ones gasp for breath, who cradle their lifeless bodies. I'm willing to wager that our collective plea of desperation resounds with the same refrain: "If you save them, I won't ever ask for anything again."

It's the metaphorical emptying of pockets, frantically searching the house for any last thing of worth you can fling onto the table in front of you, fighting like hell to satiate the beast of death to take anything, anything but this.

In that moment, for whatever reason, a miracle occurred. The kind that feels as random as the rolling of dice. Both miracle and misfortune results in us asking the same question: why me? It was as if God slowly raised his unwavering palm to the raging monster about to devour my son, commanding it to yield. The words "we've got a pulse" pierced through the air, reigniting a frenzy of activity. I glanced at Jude, who I was purposefully diverting my gaze from, and I think I took my first breath when I saw his rosy pink flesh. The team surrounded him as they tried to keep the pulse, fanning this capricious flame that no one expected to burst forth. He was immediately transferred to our larger hospital's pediatric intensive care unit (PICU) to be stabilized, and Jack and I trailed behind the ambulance. It had grown dark by the time we reached the next hospital, only 15 minutes down the road.

In the PICU, they struggled to stop Jude from deteriorating. The staff were buzzing around Jude like a hive of bees, crawling over one another, ripping open medical equipment and rolling in machines. I could only get glimpses as I stood on the sidelines. Outside his hospital room, we were introduced to a seasoned intensivist, Dr. M. He had dark eyes and was dressed casually in jeans and a sweater as he was unexpectedly called in at a late night hour. He had already administered multiple rounds of sodium bicarbonate to restore Jude's pH levels. For reasons he could not understand, nothing was stabilizing Jude's severe acidosis.

Things were getting much too crowded, so they asked us to wait outside the unit. The PICU waiting room was closed due to lingering COVID-19 precautions, so we were escorted just outside the unit into a conference room that also seemed to be utilized as a storage closet. Jack and I sat at the round, wooden conference table while a giant digital clock with the date and time glowed in red on the wall. Dr. M popped in every couple hours, but could only provide us with minimal information. They were doing their best to keep Jude alive.

We ended up having quite a long relationship with Dr. M. and, later on in our journey, he admitted to us that he initially believed Jude to be so severely neurologically compromised that both his life and ours would be nothing but suffering should he survive. Though he was not a religious man, he spent much of that night in the PICU halls praying that Jude would die.

As we waited, the chaplain that was assigned to us kept offering us food or water, but I stared silently at the wall. At some point, she placed a cup of tea on the table in front of me. She frequently stared up at the fluorescent lights in irritation, poking her head out of the room to ask nurses in the hallway if there was any way we could be placed somewhere other than this conference room. When they said they couldn't, the chaplain went to fetch us blankets in a futile attempt to provide us with some form of comfort.

After about another hour, our nurse, Julie, entered the room to check in on us. She saw Jack and I lying on the floor in the corner of the room in a makeshift bed made of hospital blankets. Julie's gaze caught the chaplain's hard glare, and they both spoke outside in the hall. A few minutes later, Julie returned and told us they had another room available. She led us into the PICU and slid open the glass doors to the first hospital room in the unit. It had a small couch in the back by a window that we could use as a bed. Another nurse walked in to hand Julie blankets, sheets, and a pillow. Behind the curtain, we overheard this nurse warn Julie that she needed to clean this up in the morning because she didn't want to get in trouble.

I was sitting stiffly on the hospital bed in the darkness

when Julie rolled in a breast pump. She asked me if I knew how to use it. I was grateful because I had been experiencing a lot of physical discomfort without breastfeeding for so many hours. I shook my head quietly and she gently taught me how to use the machine. She made it clear that I did not have to pump, but that it was an option if I wanted it. How helpful it was to have something to do, something to make me feel useful, something that connected me to my role as caretaker for my son instead of this new identity as a helpless bystander. I think she knew she was giving me that even more than she was giving me physical relief. Julie handed me plastic bottles to put the breast milk in and told me she would place it in their refrigerator. Looking back, I realized she never gave me any labels to indicate the date and time. Truthfully, this was more of a compassionate gesture. We both knew Jude would likely never need that milk.

After pumping, I laid down in bed and Jack begged me to sleep. All we could do was wait until the intensivist came back with an update on if Jude was still alive or not. It's nothing short of a miracle I was able to get even a couple hours of sleep that night, because every time I closed my eyes I saw Jude dead in my arms and I couldn't shake it out of my head. It was almost like a physical tumor I could feel in my brain. The scene was painted on the insides of my eyelids.

I fell asleep with my prayer track on repeat in my mind: Please, God. Please. Please save him. Please don't take him. Please. Please. Please.

Suddenly, around 3 a.m., my body jolted awake. I sat up straight in the dark hospital room and stared at the door — I had a feeling someone was coming. About thirty seconds later, Dr. M walked into the room. Mother's intuition, I suppose.

Jack immediately awoke, and I jumped to the edge of the bed as the doctor pulled up a chair to the bedside. The glow of the hospital lights in the hallway washed over the side of his face. We sat in the shadows together, the three of us.

Jude's condition was extremely severe, and Dr. M explained that they did not have the resources for him at this hospital, though it was a level one trauma center. He told us Jude would be transferred to CHLA (Children's Hospital of Los Angeles). I had never heard of that hospital before.

Jack asked the same question in a variety of different ways regarding Jude's chance of survival, but Dr. M couldn't answer it. He made it abundantly clear that Jude was not in good shape. Jack and I will never forget the metaphor he offered to us quietly that night.

"There may be a path ahead for your son," he told us, "but I'm sorry to say that path is through the Himalayas."

———

We left for CHLA around 4 a.m. We weren't allowed to ride in the ambulance with Jude because his condition was too severe and there was a high risk they would lose him on the way there. We drove closely behind the ambulance, never allowing it out of our sight the entire drive down.

Jack and I arrived in Los Angeles around 7 a.m. and Jude was placed in the room that was front and center of CHLA's PICU. He was alive, yes, but I had not yet understood the medical nuance that can arise in situations such as this. I still had a mind that categorized us as either alive or dead. I never considered the idea that one could be stranded somewhere in between. I never considered the irreversible damage that could occur after five minutes without oxygen, let alone half an hour or more.

Jude had a pulse as long as a machine was breathing for him, but he was in a vegetative state due to the hypoxic brain injury (lack of oxygen to the brain). In the first 24 hours, he presented as brain dead. To quote our attending doctor's clinical notes, Jude's presentation was as follows: "This patient is highly critically ill and has ongoing significant dysfunction and impairment of his neurologic and respiratory systems, such that there is a high probability of life-threatening deterioration in the patient's condition."

There was nothing to do but wait. God did not cast any illusion of control over our situation, but that doesn't mean it didn't still seep in through my skin somehow. I would be lying if there weren't days that I felt like I was confronting God as a student who had diligently prepared a failing team project, filled with questions for an absent partner. Why? Hadn't I prayed earnestly? Hadn't I humbled myself? Hadn't I made sacrifices and obeyed? Hadn't I done my part? Why didn't you fulfill your end of the deal here?

I couldn't help but think of all the time we spent praying over Jude throughout my pregnancy. I contemplated how Jack and I had carefully chosen the name Jude, which means to praise God. We had offered a prophetic prayer for Jude, envisioning a life characterized by praising God in all circumstances and a unique ability to express joy. I remembered the deliberate timing of our decision to start a family, my efforts to exercise wisdom, and even my somewhat superstitious actions, like hesitating to use body scanners at airports out of concern for their effects on pregnancy. I steered clear of caffeine, held my breath when encountering smokers on the sidewalk, and insisted on maintaining a peaceful environment to keep my stress levels low. I thought about how I chose to do all my prenatal and postpartum care through midwives to avoid hospitals, but I ended up in one for 220 days while Jude was exposed to almost daily radiation and broad-spectrum antibiotics. His skin smelled of harsh chemicals and my breast milk hung next to him in a plastic feeding bag. I felt as though I had done everything in my power to receive God's blessings, yet it seemed that, for reasons unknown, God had allowed a meteor to pierce through the atmosphere of our lives while I was busy sweeping pebbles off the front porch.

The idea that we are all-powerful gives a sense of entitlement to things that we do not hold ultimate ownership of. There is no good thing that you have earned on your own, for your very life was breathed into existence by God. It became essential for me to start each morning in the hospital with the reminder that Jude belonged to the Lord, not solely to me. He was an angel gifted to me to steward with whatever time was allotted for us. From God he came, and to God he eventually will go. Each objection to my circumstances that came to mind was like a mint placed on my tongue — I instinctively tossed it around and examined its quality, but eventually it dissolved and I was left with nothing of substance to digest.

As the human mind grapples to feel in control, it can also result in a very different emotion: guilt. If we believe that good things happen to those who do right, it can lead us to assume that bad things befall those who do wrong. My guilt over what had happened to Jude was overwhelming, particularly on that night of June 2. The inside of my mind became a criminal trial in which I was both the defendant and the jury, and the verdict was clear. I was to blame. It must have been the way I was holding him, it must've been the way his chin was positioned, it must have been the way he was pressed against me — I must've suffocated him.

When we got transferred over from the first ER room to the PICU downtown, I wouldn't stop muttering to myself that I needed to die. It wasn't necessarily because I wanted to, though that was true to some extent, but because I felt it was the natural order of things. I believed I deserved to be on death row; after all, I had killed my baby, the one being

I was supposed to protect.

I clung to this belief tightly, but with time, I tucked it away in the recesses of my mind so I could continue caring for Jude as he lay unconscious in a hospital bed. I sang to him, read books, and always held his hand. During the initial week following Jude's unexplained cardiac arrest, we conducted numerous tests. Specialists from various fields were assigned to his case, yet one by one, they all stepped down upon discovering there was nothing abnormal about their findings and nothing their particular realm of expertise could provide. The neurology team was the only one left.

Despite extensive genetic workups, metabolic testing, immunology assessments, and cardiology examinations, no test in American pediatrics could provide an explanation for what had happened to Jude or why his heart had suddenly stopped. Consequently, even our medical team felt a sense of powerlessness, which made them uneasy about the limited information they could offer. CHLA was one of the best pediatric hospitals in the country, so it was rare for them to be left so empty-handed. There was no diagnosis, no prognosis, no explanation — only a vegetative baby lying in a bed, with an uncertain chance of ever waking up. And if he did awaken, it was likely that he would be severely disabled.

I held a strong belief that cardiac arrest due to suffocation was the unspoken elephant in the room. I figured the doctors were concerned that raising this possibility might distress a postpartum, 20-something, first-time mother, who was already teetering on the brink, with blood-shot eyes and a milk-stained shirt. When word reached the staff through my husband that I suspected accidental suffocation as the cause of Jude's cardiac arrest, many of the doctors came to speak with me. They looked into my eyes and assured me that this was not the case. They explained there would have been other signs and that the medical evidence did not align with the idea of suffocation. Most importantly, they affirmed that if suffocation were indeed a serious possibility, they would have certainly informed me, as their job would require them to do so.

I nodded politely, but my sense of responsibility extended to great depths, from my brain down my spine, permeating every part of my central nervous system. I docked my boats of doubt in the harbor temporarily, but I was prepared to sail away should another hurricane blow through these waters. The human mind craves control so desperately that it will so often opt for guilt over helplessness. People say we drown in guilt, but oftentimes, it's what we use to keep us afloat.

We believe we are the ones managing our lives, both in prosperity and in adversity. We eagerly claim credit for our successes while refusing to let go of the things that were never within our control. Our brains yearn for someone to blame, for answers to the question of "why" and in my case, I had neither. I believe this tendency to seek control and assign blame is the same reason why grief and suffering can create such distance between us. You know the kind? It's what happens when people can't give you direct eye contact anymore because the demon on your shoulder digging its claws into your flesh is too distracting and terrifying to ignore. They wonder, is your pain contagious? Will it come after me next if I get too close? They're afraid of getting hypnotized by its yellow eyes, its bloody mouth, its horrifying whisper that fills the darkness with anxious thoughts when they lay their head down at night.

No one likes to be reminded that, despite our limited control, there will be times that things just happen. Tragedy pries the implicitly held just-world theory from our bony grasp. It isn't just problematic for how we view ourselves, for it is most problematic in how we view others. Much like anxiety can steal the generosity from our hearts as we obsessively secure our own comfort, the just-world theory justifies various forms of judgment and selfish ambition.

It whispers the condescending "what a shame" when the mother from down the street struggles with her teenage son who is failing classes and getting into drugs. If only she knew how to parent like you. It asks you to reconsider if the person on the corner is truly deserving of your hard-earned money. What if they just spend it on a drink? (Surely, you would never have such a vice.) It bleeds into politics by labeling who is and isn't worthy of sharing the same spaces as us, the same opportunities, the same resources. It allows disapproving looks for the parent whose child is having a meltdown in the ice cream aisle without a pause to entertain things such as learning disabilities or an overworked single parent that was given little support. It rationalizes reluctance to contribute to a fundraiser for a friend's husband who was recently diagnosed with an aggressive form of cancer. Doesn't he know smoking is carcinogenic? He should've taken his health more seriously.

Friends, the world doesn't offer us much grace. It will continue spinning regardless of what loved one you had to bury, divorce papers you had to sign, family trauma you endured, overdose you walked in on, or diagnosis you received. The last thing we need is more reasons to label people unworthy of help, compassion, or empathy. It is not a comforting truth that no amount of money or education or friends or status or shining letters of recommendation can shield you from catastrophe, but it's true nonetheless.

It seems unfortunate that some of us are confronted with this truth every time we run our fingers along our scars. We don't get to keep a comfortable distance from this reality. Blissful ignorance is a far-off memory. False hope and false security once hung above our heads like beautiful chandeliers. Perhaps they weren't true, but they sure did sparkle, casting kaleidoscopic rainbows across our walls. Now, they've shattered at our feet, glass splintering our skin and crystals sliding across the hardwood floors. We can no longer subscribe to the belief that certain events happen only to other people while sparing us — the responsible, hard-working, educated, loving, and patient people. We come to understand that such distinctions do not exist. Tragedy forces us to face our cognitive dissonance, compelling us to question our assumptions.

But maybe that's not unfortunate at all. Maybe that's the gift.

3

Trusting the One Who Takes

"Jesus was in the stern, sleeping on a cushion. The disciples woke him and said to him, 'Teacher, don't you care if we drown?'"
- Mark 4:38 (NIV)

If you were a god and gathered a group of people to be your followers, what defining characteristic would you desire in them? How would you label them? Perhaps as people who praise you, or people who love you, or people who obey you, or maybe even just people who believe in you. In the Bible, God's people are referred to as "the Israelites," as they all descend from Jacob, whose name was later changed to Israel. The word "Israel" means to wrestle with God, a concept I always found interesting. God chooses to characterize his people as those who struggle with him, as those who fight him. Is that not an integral part of faith?

Faith is too often equated with merely believing in something, having hope, or maintaining a positive mindset. While Jude spent week after week at CHLA, only presenting as mildly conscious, many people reminded me to have faith. Although I agreed with the importance of faith, I feared it might be an illusive, blurry concept that held a different meaning for each of us. Sometimes I wanted to ask, "Faith in what? What exactly are you asking me to have faith in?"

Faith can be used as a beautiful quilt carefully laid

over a messy bed, seen as a way to avoid confronting the ugly aspects of life. Some refer to this as spiritual bypassing, using religion as a means to escape the reality of psychological wounds or suppressing emotional needs. This faith tells you that God is good, therefore he will see to it that all of us enjoy a long, beautiful life with the three bedroom house and the healthy children and the great job promotion — at least, those in developed nations with a comfortable salary.

The truth is, babies die. Kids get sick. Accidents happen. People fail. Life isn't fair, and anyone who gets close enough to God is bound to have a full out wrestling match with him at some point or another. The dust kicks up all around us while we hurl our painful questions out with each strike to his chest: "How could you? Where are you? Don't you care at all?"

As the days went by, Jude did begin to show signs of recovery, but slowly. In fact, one of the doctors said if Jude were to ever wake up, it should be classified as the slowest recovery of all time. We eventually managed to extubate him after 10 days, but there was ongoing debate among our medical team regarding whether we should be weaning his breathing support, and some were even questioning whether he was displaying consciousness at all. In this season, I didn't always know what it looked like to have faith. It's easier to communicate to a God who's transactional, but I had to communicate to a God whom I believed had the power to heal but I could observe enough of the world to know he rarely operated as a genie-in-a-bottle.

Here's what faith was not: it wasn't ignoring the reality I was in. It wasn't donning rose-colored glasses. It wasn't the ability to see life from a bird's-eye view, affording me a perspective in which everything makes sense. It wasn't insisting that God has no business in such misery. It wasn't assigning promises never made to a God who does not make our comfort his number one priority. It wasn't believing that if I prayed enough, if I believed enough, if I put enough coins in the proverbial gumball machine, they'd come pouring out. It wasn't a means to fit a traumatic event neatly in my mind. Having faith didn't mean I disregarded the season I was in, nor did it mean I intentionally ignored reason and evidence. That's not what my child needed. He needed me to be there, right there, in the dark and dire. And indeed, it was dire.

During the first week, Jude showed no signs of consciousness. The neurology team, whom I referred to as "the dark cloud," frequently examined him for reflexes. I must clarify that it was nothing like the gentle reflex hammer tap you might experience at a pediatrician's appointment. They dug their nails into his cuticles, pinched him forcefully enough to leave him covered in bruises, brushed cotton swabs over his corneas, and inserted instruments down his throat to elicit a gag. We engaged in difficult conversations almost daily about when doctors would recommend withdrawing care — which, by the way, is not as airbrushed as certain euphemisms might allude to. There was no plug to pull; the reality was that we would stop supplying milk to his feeding pump, and Jude would slowly starve to death. It would require us to step back and allow his organs to fail.

Faith is not synonymous with hope. Faith is believing that God will do what he said he would do. This will prove challenging if you think God promised a whole lot of things he never promised. I'll spare you from yet another rant against the prosperity gospel, but in our society's pursuit of greater abundance, wealth, and material comforts, we have an especially hard time accepting anything other than a good time. Faith is an exercise of remembering, and I use the word "exercise" intentionally. It doesn't come naturally to engage our minds and consider truth that lies beyond our senses, but it requires us to utilize reason rather than to abandon it. It asks us to seek evidence, not to ignore it.

To have faith is to seek evidence for the light when the presence of darkness is unbearably self-evident. Faith demands that we remember. What did God say? What has he done? Is he trustworthy? When you find the strength to answer these questions, you need to cling to them for dear life — because you're in it. The storm is here. You will need something to keep you afloat that is separate from your circumstances. I did not need to ignore the very real and likely possibility that my son would not survive, I needed to consider the God who gave me my son in the first place.

Faith is about bearing witness to the darkness surrounding you while finding the strength, courage, and reason to believe that, although you cannot see the sun, you know it's there. When you are accustomed to sleeping peacefully through the night, it's easy to navigate through the darkness. All you've known is closing your eyes one moment and opening them to sunlight the next. But when your mind, body, and soul are unable to rest, tormented minute by minute, when horrifying hallucinations dance across the walls and feed on your fears, you're going to start to doubt if dawn is coming. You will begin to realize that the night never felt this long before. You're going to keep glancing at the clock, heart racing, teeth chattering, adrenaline pumping, and wonder when this hell is going to end. You're going to keep wandering about, disoriented and blind in the darkness. The light switches won't work, you'll hear whispers and maniacal laughter in the shadows, you'll try to scream but no noise will escape your lips, and you'll feel like a child trapped in a nightmare you can't awaken from. The fear will be real and it will be valid. You will forget what sunlight feels like, what its warmth is like against your skin. You'll have a million reasons to start theorizing that something has gone terribly wrong and perhaps morning may never come.

This is when you must have faith. You must reason. You must remember. You must engage your mind, pull out the astronomy textbooks, and refresh yourself on the truth. The truth is, the Earth is spinning on its rotational axis at approximately 1,000 miles per hour. The sun is the center of our solar system and it hasn't gone anywhere, not for the last 4.5 billion years. I know you can't always feel it, you can't always see it, but it's still shining. It does not disappear while the world is asleep.

This is also the truth: though the sunlight is on its way, it doesn't diminish the length of the night. It doesn't make it any less cold. It doesn't make it any less dark. It doesn't stop the terror. But, it encourages you to rummage through the junk drawer and find the compass. It reminds you to walk in faith towards the west-facing window in your house. It guides your gaze to the horizon, knowing that the sun will once again come into view. Faith enables us to experience what we hope for, the thing that has not yet come. It allows us to navigate the in-between, the unknown, the darkness, and the fear.

One biblical story that weighed heavily on my husband's and my minds at the beginning of our hospital journey was the story of Abraham and Isaac in the book of Genesis. God promises Abraham numerous descendants, but he and his wife, Sarah, struggle to conceive. As the years pass, it appears to them that God might not fulfill his end of the deal. Doubts surely crept into their minds. Did we misunderstand his message? Did he truly make that promise? Was he merely speaking metaphorically?

Feeling that heaven had gone silent, Abraham and Sarah take matters into their own hands to conceive, but their efforts fall short. Eventually, God grants them Isaac, from whom countless generations will come. God has proven himself faithful. He has answered their prayers. Until shortly after, when God asks Abraham to surrender his son to him. Yes, the very son through whom God promised numerous descendants is called to die. So, Abraham is in quite a predicament. It doesn't seem like God's plan is realistic. How can Abraham be the father of many nations when his only son dies?

Despite this, Abraham exercises faith. He remembers who God is. He knows that life will continually supply him an endless conveyor belt of circumstances that fill him with fear, but he must hold steadfast to an absolute truth that remains unaltered by what he sees, experiences, or comprehends. He becomes the physicist who must infer the existence of dark matter, even though he cannot detect it. Abraham decides that, in some way, God will resolve this apparent contradiction. Hebrews 11:19 tells us that Abraham *reasoned* that God could raise the dead back to life. Even in the face of death, Abraham could trust him.

Jack and I knew that God might take Jude, and although that was a painful and frightening thought, the very circumstance we were put in demonstrated how little you can trust your own perception of the world. We experienced first-hand how dramatically our perspective can change and how helpless we really are. What does not change, however, is God. Though we could not have faith in any particular circumstance or desired outcome, we could put faith in a God who is true to his word.

This is the faith that gave us the strength to attend every early morning round and immerse ourselves in medical jargon until we became fluent. It gave us the strength to consider letting Jude go should he only suffer. It gave us the strength to advocate for Jude should he thrive. It gave me the strength to continue pumping milk every two hours around the clock to provide him food. It gave us the strength to show up instead of shrink back. That did not mean we did not petition in prayer everyday. That did not mean we did not hope for better. Yes, we obediently marched our son to the top of the mountain for sacrifice, but we pleaded every step of the way.

We reminded God: you are good, you do not delight in the death of the innocent. Surely, you do not want this. Surely, not my firstborn son. Will you not provide another sacrifice? Will you not reconsider?

—

Weeks passed by. We were still at CHLA, and it was starting to become evident to us that Jude's stay was far longer than usual. We were frequently bouncing between rooms in the back of the unit, often ending up in shared rooms with views of concrete buildings and minimal attention. I only left Jude's side if he was sleeping, but there were times when I returned to find him crying and covered in his own vomit. I don't fault the staff for this, they simply cannot be everywhere at once. Still, it only strengthened my belief that I could never leave him. Specialists were visiting us less and less, for there are only so many ways to phrase "I don't know."

I grew exhausted of hearing the same thing every morning when we met with the team. I became so desperate for information, I was willing to accept any crumbs of insight I could gather off the floors. I implored the doctors to stop reciting politically correct scripts and give me their honest opinions on Jude's prognosis. Many continued to dance around the question for fear of saying anything that they could not prove, but the ones who recognized my need took pity on me. Knowing I needed something, anything, they admitted that they did not personally believe Jude would ever recover. Their words drew blood, but bleeding was better than drowning in the silence.

We were tossed about like rag dolls at the mercy of the waves. Some days, people were optimistic about Jude, while on others, the hopelessness felt palpable. It was a constant cycle of reopening wounds, never allowing a scab to form. It was one of the most unnatural, horrendous spaces to exist in.

Nearly a month into our stay, Jude was transferred to CHLA's NICU. Many people had questioned why Jude was not initially in the NICU, and it was because neonates are typically only admitted to the NICU immediately after birth. The NICU avoids accepting babies who have gone home due to the risk of introducing illness to the most vulnerable population. Thus, when Jude was transferred to CHLA, he moved from our local hospital's PICU to their PICU, as it was essentially a transfer from one unit to another. PICU stays are typically brief, as only the most critical patients are stabilized there before being moved to surgery or a discharge floor. Tragically, there is a high fatality rate in these units. Many children sent to a large PICU like CHLA's did not survive.

Once again, we were stuck somewhere in the in-between. Jude was no longer presenting as brain dead, he was slightly improving each week, but the progress was microscopic and debatable at best. What complicated matters even further was that Jude's EEGs (which monitor brain activity) and MRIs (which they expected to reveal strokes throughout his cortex and brain stem) came back normal. Our neurologists were clearly thrown for a loop, but consistently reminded us that, even though they couldn't explain the normal brain scans, Jude must have undoubtedly suffered damage. So you see, we are all people of faith, affirming truths for which our limited insights may not gather sufficient evidence for.

In the NICU, we began staying at the Ronald McDonald house overnight. The timing worked out well because we started sleeping there right when Jude began sleeping at night. Up until that point, we slept in Jude's hospital room by his bed because his sleep/wake cycles had not normalized. He was completely unresponsive in the days but wide awake and highly agitated at night. Jack and I naturally fell into a rhythm of Jack taking night shift and switching off with me around 5 a.m. Jude had experienced something known as "neurostorming" in the beginning, which commonly occurs after brain injuries. The brain struggles to regulate all of its systems like the central nervous system, sympathetic nervous system, and parasympathetic nervous system. One can become overly sensitive to stimulation and experience extreme and acute stress. Jude's eyes would be locked on the ceiling, wide with panic. Even though he couldn't move, his heart rate soared, his blood pressure spiked, and his breathing became erratic as his chest heaved. It was god awful to witness. He was in pain, terrified, trapped in his own body and there was nothing I could do to help.

One particular night, Jude's vitals were alarmingly high, and he was convulsing. He wasn't even responding to Ativan. The doctors ended up administering too many doses in a desperate attempt to calm him, which caused Jude's blood pressure to plummet to dangerously low levels. They had to give him emergency bolus, which subsequently led to abnormally low hemoglobin levels, triggering further chaos as they feared internal bleeding in his brain. Ours was the most hectic room in the unit that night with doctors flooding in, alarms blaring incessantly as Jude's vitals ran haywire. I clung to Jack's sleeve, bracing myself to hear the news that Jude was gone. The nightmare persisted for hours until we could conclusively rule out hemorrhaging and stabilize Jude's blood pressure and hemoglobin levels through a blood transfusion in the morning.

The NICU is where Jude finally began to make noise. We used to pray and pray we would hear him cry again, and then he never stopped. As more weeks passed, Jude gradually became more alert. However, the more he awakened, the more pain he realized he was in. Some of Jude's NICU rooms would be more accurately referred to as closets because there were no windows and you could barely open the door to the room with how much equipment surrounded his tiny bed. For about a month, from sun up to sun down, Jude was crying. His cry was weak and hoarse. He struggled to breathe, gurgling on the mucus he couldn't swallow. He had so much mucus you could hear the gurgling cry down the hall. He was being sustained by heavy respiratory tubing that tugged on his face and served as both life support but also a painful tether. The room was dimly lit by the soft glow of machines, so it looked like it was perpetually 3 a.m. We rarely saw the light of day. For 14 hour stretches, we were confined to this small hospital room with our screaming baby without relief. Nurses pleaded with us to step out and get some rest, but I would never leave him. Sometimes the doctors prescribed morphine when his blood pressure raised high enough to indicate he must be in severe pain. I am certain there is no greater hell than watching your child suffer.

Jude had an NJ feeding tube, which meant that it went from his nostril to his intestines, bypassing his stomach to prevent the risk of aspiration. Since Jude could not cough or swallow, he had recurrent collapsed lungs from the secretions he couldn't manage. The last thing he needed was a lung infection, so aspiration could be fatal. Diagnosing lung infections was challenging because Jude's chest x-rays consistently showed white where you ought to see black in a healthy x-ray. The white appearance on his imaging was due to the collapse of his lungs. As a result, he was often put on potent, broad-spectrum antibiotics just in case.

Though Jude couldn't cough effectively, his body compensated by performing a peculiar and painful-looking heaving motion to clear his throat, almost like vomiting. Our pulmonologist believed it was his way of using his abdomen to mimic a cough because he could no longer build pressure in his thoracic cavity. This heave sounded incredibly uncomfortable and was always followed by tears. On the unlucky days, the heaves were forceful enough to dislodge his feeding tube from his intestines. There were also occasions the heaving caused Jude's dislodged feeding tube to continue traveling upwards, coiling in his esophagus, spewing milk, and no one knew until we would spot it on one of his x-rays when trying to determine the cause of his agitation and breathing difficulty.

Those weeks in the NICU remain etched in my memory as one of the darkest periods of my life, both literally and figuratively.

In July, our neurologist visited us again. She had been one of the few to remain optimistic about Jude. I believe it was because she couldn't shake the fact that he had normal brain activity and no observable structural damage. When Jude first showed signs of consciousness, she believed he would make a full recovery in a matter of months.

When she walked into our room, we jumped to our feet. We hadn't seen her in several weeks, as she wanted to give Jude more time. She conducted her usual assessment, checked for reflexes that were absent, and stood silently in our windowless room. Nothing demanded our attention quite like the presence of a neurologist. They are professional bad news bearers, so when their words inevitably cause the ground beneath you to disintegrate, all you have left to grab onto with dear life is their words hanging in the air.

She gently told us that Jude was not recovering

as expected or hoped. His muscle tone was high, causing stiffness in his legs and his arms to curl tightly against his body. He didn't track objects well, failed to respond to loud sounds, and still displayed no cough, gag, swallow, suck, or startle reflexes. This was the first time she unofficially mentioned his diagnosis: spastic cerebral palsy.

I didn't fully grasp what this meant for Jude, and I didn't have the capacity to find out. My eyes glazed over and my throat closed shut while Jack began a frantic and hopeless conversation about how this colored Jude's future. I fixed my gaze on the shadows dancing on the wall and concentrated on the sound of the ventilator providing Jude with breaths as our neurologist shared her concerns. She believed Jude was likely blind, and possibly also deaf. Although we had occasionally seen him track objects for a moment, her somber presence made every glimmer of hope look like a trick of the light, a deluded dream we wished to be true. Jack asked if this meant Jude would never walk, talk, eat, or engage with us on any level. The neurologist could only shrug helplessly. With such little information to guide her, she admitted that all these concerns were valid, and strong possibilities we needed to seriously consider.

She apologized once more for her initial assessment of him. Now that we were over a month out from the original injury, Jude's severely poor presentation proved to her that he was worse off than she had originally thought. That day felt like we finally smacked the concrete from whatever building we fell off of months ago. For the first time since Jude's cardiac arrest, I couldn't hold back my tears. I had lost the ability to speak. Pushing past the neurologist, I ran downstairs to sob into my knees in some secluded corner of the hospital.

I didn't know what God expected of me. I felt I had extended the olive branch to him. I had come to terms with the possibility that Jude might not survive. I had mustered the courage to surrender my son. I had been rational and understanding. All I asked for in return was that Jude not endure unnecessary suffering. (I had not yet understood that humans will perceieve almost all suffering to be unnecessary suffering.) It seemed like God was using my worst fears against me, and I couldn't understand him for that.

Jude's life was an unending cycle of pain. He was drowning in his own bodily fluids and his delicate skin had become covered in scars and bruises from countless medical procedures. Catheters were forcefully inserted through his nose and mouth into his trachea for deep airway suctioning every few hours, even while he slept. All we wanted was for Jude to be conscious, and now he was, but only as a torturous medical experiment. He didn't ever experience the comfort of a peaceful bed, the soothing embrace of his mother, a full stomach, or the sight of sunlight flickering through the trees. His life was a living hell, and with no medical answers, no one could tell me if it would ever end.

We were living in boundless darkness. No one could offer us a narrative, definitive statements, or even a plan for treatment. There was no horizon, only limitless fears that demanded to be impossibly and simultaneously entertained. We couldn't orient ourselves because there were no stars to guide us. Life had become a terrible nightmare and we found no comfort in morning whispers that it was but a dream. Instead, there was only the same bleak response echoing across the black abyss:

"Perhaps so,

Perhaps so."

4

Things That May Never Come

"Seventy years are given to us! Some even live to eighty. But even the best years are filled with pain and trouble; soon they disappear, and we fly away."
- Psalms 90:10 (NLT)

As the weeks passed in the NICU, more tests were done. Jude's genetic workup all came back normal. We did a third MRI, just to rule out what they call pseudo-normalization, but it yielded the same results. Our neurologist scrutinized the scans, desperate to find a sign that matched Jude's physical presentation. She focused her study on his basal ganglia (the part of the brain responsible for motor control) due to its sensitivity to lack of oxygen and Jude's motor issues. She thought she detected a subtle decrease in volume but wasn't certain if it was due to differences in resolution between scans. She consulted the radiologist, resulting in a debate over the minutiae of pixels. Ultimately, the radiologist concluded this was an absolutely normal MRI scan with no volume decrease in any areas of the brain, and he would not be convinced otherwise. Part of me always wondered what that conversation was like, and if our neurologist was pleading, *"There has to be something, if you could only see how bad this kid looks..."*

Muscle tone issues are a very common result of hypoxic brain injuries, typically presenting as increased tone in the limbs and decreased tone in the trunk. This means arm and leg muscles can become tight because the brain isn't sending the signal to stop flexing, and the neck and throat area can lose muscle tone, becoming floppy. In cases like this, people may need to be strapped into a wheelchair because they don't have the core strength to hold themselves upright. Additionally, people with these issues often require a tracheostomy (a surgically placed artificial windpipe) because their floppy upper airway tissues could obstruct breathing. Our neurologist was almost certain Jude had decreased trunk muscle tone, which would explain why he was struggling so much with secretion management and respiratory distress.

"I know his airway is floppy," she told us. "If it's not, I'd be stumped."

Multiple scope examinations revealed that Jude had a structurally normal airway, confounding the medical team. His vocal chords weren't paralyzed and his epiglottis moved normally. Had our team found what they were looking for, the next step would have been standard procedure; they would have officially recommended a trach for Jude. They made it abundantly clear that muscle tone issues due to brain injuries were permanent, and it wasn't anything we could expect to get better with time. Now that Jude's poor airway protection seemed to be more of a coordination issue and less of a muscle tone issue, it colored Jude's future in even more uncertainty. Maybe it would get better in time, but maybe it wouldn't — and airways aren't exactly things doctors are comfortable taking a gamble on.

In the meantime, we continued on with the long and slow process of trying to wean Jude completely off his ventilator. Patients cannot be removed from the ICU if they are still dependent on a machine to breathe, so the next step was to see how far we could push Jude. If he ever had a hint of an infection or any drop in his oxygen (commonly referred to as a "desat"), we lost all his progress and put him back on full support. It was one step forward, ten steps back. What was most stressful is that we did not know if the finish line even existed. There was no guarantee we would ever be able to wean Jude off the ventilator.

As Jude woke up more, he cried less frequently and needed less breathing support. Eventually, they transferred us to a room with a window, and I couldn't have been more grateful to see even a little daylight. Even if the view was a slab of concrete, I was content with a dull, gray reflection of the sun. Funny how your perspective changes.

By the end of July, after two months in the ICU, Jude was taken off his ventilator. I couldn't contain my excitement to see this progress, regardless of how long it took. He was still receiving oxygen, but now we knew he could breathe on his own. The NICU staff barely waited a day before transferring him onto the discharge floor, a move we were not expecting to happen so soon. If he wasn't on breathing support, he was automatically deemed more stable than everyone else in the ICU, and they had other patients who needed the bed.

The more Jude developed, the more optimism he received from the medical staff. He began moving his limbs a little more, holding his head up, tracking more consistently, stretching, and even giving small smiles. We were overjoyed to be sent to the discharge floor and out of the ICU, thinking we were closer than ever to going home. Unfortunately, Jude did have an immediate desat episode the night they transferred him and was almost sent back to the ICU. He ended up normalizing with the help of more oxygen, but Jude continued to face challenges with his respiratory instability that kept everyone on their toes. Chest x-rays often showed "severe atelectasis," where lung air sacs have collapsed, causing Jude's oxygen saturation levels (SpO2) to frequently drop into the 80s.

We were assigned a new pulmonologist on the discharge floor. She studied at John Hopkins and always wore a pristine white lab coat. Her perfectly curled and highlighted blonde hair bounced when she walked across the hospital floor to assess Jude. A shiny stethoscope always hung from her neck and her fingernails were always polished, usually pink. Like all the other respiratory therapists that checked Jude's lungs every couple hours, she commented on how his lungs sounded like a washing machine. Although Jude's gurgling had improved, his breathing was terribly noisy as air struggled to flow in and out. It was not uncommon for his skin to be tugging in between his ribs while he fought to breathe. The pulmonologist always gave Jude the most heartbreaking, pitiful looks which did anything but encourage us. Like many others, she dangled the possibility of a trach in our faces almost every day, but we were still holding out hope.

In August, on Jack's 26th birthday, our pulmonologist came to visit us as she did every morning. We smiled and chatted with her, unaware of the bomb she was about to drop. She sat down with us and officially gave us her professional recommendation: she did not believe Jude could leave the hospital without a trach. She believed him to be unfit to manage his own secretions and was concerned about his ability to gain weight due to the immense energy he had to expend on breathing. It was the kind of conversation that left you sick to your stomach the rest of the day.

She spoke of worst-case scenarios with us, explaining that Jude's lung health may deteriorate for the rest of his life. The damage to his lungs would become permanent and, if Jude survived the next few years, we may need to surgically remove one of his lungs. These were all abstract possibilities that were difficult for my brain to entertain without spiraling into despair, but she shared them in hopes we would consider the potential benefits of a trach.

I knew the decision about a trach was one of the major conversations that needed to be had before we could move forward in Jude's hospitalization. The likelihood that I would get to take Jude home at all used to be slim, but now that he was off a ventilator, I got a second wind. I was starting to believe there was a chance Jude could survive. Whether or not he needed a trach became the big question. I had prayed against a trach desperately almost everyday. It had become my most recited, determined plea. Especially with the complete lack of information about what we could expect for Jude's future, a trach seemed to be a symbol of the severity of his brain damage and what it might mean for his quality of life.

Not to mention, a tracheostomy was a significant intervention, not without its risks and side effects. It heightened the risk of mucus plugs and lung infections, which could lead to permanent scarring or death. Moreover, it posed a formidable obstacle to Jude's oral coordination and abilities, effectively robbing him of the ability to speak or cry. Given Jude's global developmental delay and the challenges he already faced, I hated the thought of intentionally adding more hurdles to his path that he may never overcome. It was a heart-wrenching dilemma as he had grown to exhibit improved motor function, tracked our movements, smiled, and interacted with his surroundings, yet struggled with the fundamental reflexes necessary to protect his own life.

Jack and I found ourselves devastated and frustrated, not only because of the bad news we had received but also due to the ever-shifting opinions depending on which medical professional we spoke to. Some doctors were convinced that Jude unquestionably needed a tracheostomy, while others argued it was unjustifiable and that any child truly requiring one wouldn't have survived long enough to debate its necessity for months on end.

Our hospital room was shared, separated by a curtain, and shortly after we received this unsettling recommendation, another patient with a trach was transferred into our room. I hadn't intended to eavesdrop, but I couldn't help but notice the frequent suctioning procedures the poor girl underwent by both the respiratory therapists and her parents. She was getting suctioned even more than Jude was, and Jude needed suctioning every minute. As I pondered what course of action would be best for Jude, something about the idea of a tracheostomy didn't sit right with me. While some medical staff assured us that a trach would make things easier, it appeared to me that it would introduce more complexities and risks into Jude's already complicated medical situation.

What it unquestionably did was make *their* jobs easier. It provided an artificial, secure airway for a patient with chronic and acute respiratory failure. From my perspective, this new variable might not only fail to solve Jude's problems but could actually exacerbate them. Considering Jude's pre-existing struggles with secretion management, I questioned the wisdom of surgically introducing a foreign object into his trachea, something that would certainly increase mucus production. A trach seemed to be a medical intervention that would aid other medical interventions, but I feared that would place us in a never-ending cycle that could completely diminish any quality of life for Jude in the pursuit of keeping him alive.

With these concerns at the forefront of my mind, I requested a family meeting during morning rounds the next day. I felt it was unfair that communication had become so inconsistent, although I recognized how easily that could happen across different units and among various specialists. I also requested the presence of a palliative care team at the meeting to have support in advocating for Jude's quality of life. I wanted the meeting to encompass more than just brainstorming medical interventions for a long-term patient no one knew what to do with.

Just when it began to feel like it was about to be us against the entire medical team, God sent us a small encouragement. A respiratory therapist who had cared for Jude during his time in the PICU months ago happened to be assigned to our roommate on the discharge floor. When he walked in the room and saw us, he immediately threw his hands up and ran over to us. He was overjoyed to see us again, as many of the PICU staff don't ever know what becomes of their most severe patients. This particular respiratory therapist was once seen crying by Jack in the nurses' station the day he extubated Jude. He had prepared himself for Jude to fail the moment we took him off invasive breathing support, so Jude's success was overwhelming for him.

As someone who was shocked Jude survived extubation, he was particularly happy to find Jude holding his own head up and tracking each movement with his big blue eyes. He was curious about the reason for the delay in Jude's progress when he had already overcome so much. We explained Jude's breathing difficulties, chronic lung disease, and the recent recommendation for a tracheostomy from our pulmonologist. The respiratory therapist stared at us with a lifted brow, turned his head behind his shoulder, and pulled the curtain across the room before walking back to us. It was almost as if he was going to share a confidential medical revelation.

In hushed tones, he leaned against Jude's bedside railing. He urged us to hold off on the tracheostomy for as long as possible. Drawing from his experience with tracheostomy patients, he shared his belief that it would be detrimental to Jude. He argued that it wouldn't resolve the issues at hand but would rather put Jude at an even higher risk of infection and mucus plugging. It was a relief to hear a trained medical professional arrive at the same conclusions I had.

After that day, I decided to utilize every spare moment I had in the hospital to conduct extensive research. I delved into highly respected medical journals, watched videos of parents whose children had trachs, and absorbed every piece of advice, every account of unforeseen complications, every praise report, and every relevant medical study. My quest for knowledge encompassed not only the surgical procedure itself but also the intricacies of maintenance and cleaning, the potential side effects, and the typical medical rationale behind most tracheostomy procedures. I was well-versed in the lives it had saved, but I also knew the stories of the infections, the deaths, and the challenging decannulation processes.

To organize my findings and prepare for the upcoming family meeting, I had a little red notebook that served as a repository for relevant medical literature. I also jotted down the questions I intended to pose to the medical staff. If they were going to suggest a life-altering surgery that required my informed consent, I was going to demand the information I needed to consent. Though I knew it would weigh heavily on my mind if our entire medical team agreed that a trach would be the safest way to move forward, I was not going to simply take their word for it. I was going to make my case — they should be prepared to make theirs.

On August 9, Jack and I squeezed into a cramped storage room alongside Jude's medical team. The other conference room was occupied, and there were too many people on Jude's case to fit comfortably in his hospital room. Our nurse brought in additional chairs, and we found ourselves in a cluttered, fluorescent-lit room filled with miscellaneous supplies, our palliative care team, a neurologist, our pulmonologist, our attending doctor, our residents, and a speech and dysphagia specialist.

Our pulmonologist initiated the discussion, providing a general overview of Jude's severe respiratory complications. As she approached the topic we had all convened to address — the potential tracheostomy — I clutched my red notebook in my pocket, ready to use it as a weapon in this battle for Jude's life. My heart raced, and just as I began to bring the notebook onto my lap, preparing to present my arguments, I heard astonishing words that left me in stunned silence: "We do not recommend a tracheostomy at this time."

My eyes locked onto our pulmonologist in disbelief, and I glanced over at the palliative care team, who shared our astonishment. As our pulmonologist explained the reasoning behind their decision, I wondered if she had somehow gotten a hold of my notebook while I slept because she hit nearly all the counterarguments I had meticulously noted. The attending doctor chimed in, explaining that they had collectively concluded that a tracheostomy would likely introduce more risks than benefits and that there was no evidence it would resolve Jude's current issues. I fumbled through my notebook of defense for a point that was already won, trying to gather new thoughts for this unexpected turn. Smiles grew across our faces and our emotions shifted from anxious anticipation to elated optimism, a rare and beautiful flower that hardly ever grew among those sterile hospital walls.

At some point, that optimism seemed to fill the air with an aroma our pulmonologist couldn't ignore. She sternly reminded us multiple times that she might still recommend a tracheostomy for Jude in the future. Pediatric doctors of critically ill children are so accustomed to managing the unrealistic hopes that parents refuse to let go of. As a self-proclaimed realist, I never considered myself to be someone easily carried away in the clouds, but today, I was not sliding my feet into those cement blocks. I was elated at the news, and I allowed myself to feel genuinely hopeful for the first time.

—

The discharge floor held a promising buoyancy that brought me relief. In the ICU, where mortality rates were high, the air was thick with an unsettling silence. It was silent like a brain bleed. The only sounds were from the ventilators artificially filling lungs with oxygen. On the discharge floor, we heard children crying. We saw them in their hospital gowns walking up and down the halls, rolling their medical poles beside them. Sick children in the hospital seem like they would be sad images, but for us, all we saw were signs of life. Signs that they weren't unconscious or severely brain damaged or completely bedridden. Here, there was an expectation of recovery, even if it was only partial.

I was split between rejoicing in how far Jude had come and clinging to the walls for dear life because of how paranoid I was that some tornado would rip through the doorway and toss him back to the ICU at any moment. Jude never fit cleanly into any categories for anyone, and it was no different when it came to making decisions about whether he was stable enough to be on the discharge floor. Every move our medical team made seemed to be riddled with hesitancy, regardless of how well they tried to drape over it with confidence.

Now that we had come to a conclusion regarding the trach, we could finally set our sights on where to go from here. There was a checklist of tasks to complete before Jude could finally go home, and the mere consideration of working on that list filled me with a sense of hope. Jude's to-do list included a gastrostomy tube (g-tube) surgery for feeding and a sleep study.

At this point, Jude was consistently tracking and staring down everyone who entered his hospital room, alleviating most concerns about his eyesight. However, they did give him a hearing test which showed that he had severe hearing loss. Thankfully, they believed this was due to severe congestion and fluid build-up in his ear canals rather than neurological damage. It could be solved with ear tubes which we could surgically place during his g-tube procedure. They also needed the sleep study to assess Jude's oxygen requirements during sleep and monitor any apneic episodes he may be having.

It never seemed that too many good things could happen at once, and Jude began getting fevers. While atelectasis could sometimes cause fevers, his soaring heart rate raised concerns. Chest x-rays were of little help because it was too challenging to distinguish between Jude's typical lung condition and an actual lung infection. Given the other infection markers he was presenting with, our medical team decided to treat him for pneumonia. Each time we had to treat Jude for an infection was devastating because it meant there would be absolutely no progress for at least the next 10-14 days. I hated treating him for infections we didn't even know for certain if he had, but to make the wrong choice could be fatal. I knew the risks of such frequent antibiotic use, but I could not afford the luxury of protecting my child from every danger. I had to pick and choose which poison he must drink. And so, Jude went back on antibiotics.

When each and every waking hour of your life is staring at a hospital wall, hearing that you needed to wait another day was torture — let alone two weeks. It was almost an abstract to me, like saying I needed to wait 100 years. There was nothing else on our to-do list we could tackle in the meantime. The presence of an infection rendered a sleep study invalid, as it wouldn't provide an accurate reflection of Jude's baseline oxygen requirements. Moreover, pediatric surgery would never operate on an unstable infant with a lung infection. Once again, we could do nothing but wait.

Jude turned three months old in the hospital. Apart from his chronic lung disease, Jude continued to defy expectations. His muscle tone improved, making it possible to incorporate physical therapies into his routine. Prior to this progress, he was in such discomfort that he couldn't get through any therapy sessions without crying or desatting if you placed him in the wrong position. Even the music therapists couldn't calm him with a wagon full of beautiful instruments. His improved limb mobility surprised us, considering earlier predictions that his increased muscle tone would be permanent and possibly worsen over time. Although our most recent neurologist had indicated that Jude would likely have a walking disability, our therapists were starting to believe it was too early to make such determinations.

Jack's mom often dropped off some clothes for Jude, and for the first time, I began dressing him in normal clothes instead of hospital gowns. It took me three months to allow myself this small joy. I could finally begin entertaining the idea that Jude might be a baby on his way out of the hospital, rather than a long-term patient who would likely never leave the hospital. I always had a difficult time mixing things I deemed "bad" and "good" together. It was almost like a perfectionist side of me. If something was categorized as "bad," I just allowed it to be so. I did not try to throw light in with darkness because I believed the darkness would overcome it. I feared it would leave its stain on everything. I didn't want Jude's baby clothes to be tainted. I didn't want hope. I didn't want an illusion of redemption. I wasn't going to try and salvage normalcy because nothing about this was normal. It was a tragedy. To dress it up would be like preparing a body for a viewing. To me, death was not as disturbing as the artificial attempt to mask it.

Even though I was grateful my son was still alive, the 22nd of every month that marked another month of his life spent in the hospital made me sick. I couldn't help but envy all the normal moms who had the ability to celebrate each month's milestones. Normal moms' tears fall in the bittersweet realizations that their little baby isn't a little baby anymore. Normal moms joke that they wish their babies would just never grow up, a well-meaning cliche that I will always flinch at, knowing all too well that it is nothing short of a privilege to watch your child grow up. Normal moms do not consider milestones to be miracles.

Not only did Jude have an uphill battle regarding his development due to a severe brain injury, but I became overwhelmed thinking about the consequences that might come from a three-month-old who has never left his bed. I did everything I could to stimulate him through songs, books, and games. I played him the sounds of birds chirping and rain pattering on the roof. I told him all about trees and butterflies and flowers. I asked him to hang on long enough so I could show him the ocean.

Every morning, I arrived at the hospital around 7 a.m. and immediately held him, whispering prayers of gratitude to God that he made it through the night. I placed sticky notes on the TV next to the hospital bed that kindly asked the staff not to exercise screen time with Jude. Anything and everything that even had a chance at hindering his development was strictly off-limits. I kissed his face and tummy and feet so he knew the sensation of something other than needles digging under his skin when we needed to run blood labs or penetrating catheters when we needed urine samples. I needed him to know life wasn't all pain.

But, the thing is — life is pain. It is astounding and it is awful, it is divine and it is devastating. Initially, I could not see the point in embracing what little light remained. It resembled a fragile candle destined to be extinguished by life's harshest winds. While we acknowledge and honor our pain, we must find the courage to crack the shutters, both for ourselves and for those who are too weak to do so themselves. The light may only cast a faint glow on a small part of your story, but you will learn that joy and sadness grow in the same field. To know one, you must experience the other. This can be profoundly difficult when life unfolds contrary to our expectations. The grief for what should have been can consume us entirely, depriving us the chance to discover joy and hope amidst the sorrow. If an unwelcome diagnosis, disease, or devastating event tears into the pages of our story, it becomes crucial to remember: the journey of healing is rarely linear. It is not a viable strategy to wait for a return to normalcy. Tragedies have a way of pushing us over a bridge that immediately crumbles into the canyon below, leaving us stranded somewhere we never wanted to be.

As long as life endures, gratitude will grow where it is watered. There is some flickering star to be found if you would only look up. Hope remains within reach. For me, it took several months before I humbly engaged with blessings I previously disregarded as unrecognizable in the wake of my grief — and that's okay. You can take your time. Just know that if you are waiting for remission, for more than three good days in a row, for a full recovery — these things may never come. Don't throw away what glitters just because it isn't gold. I needed those small moments of blessing, even though they were so much smaller than what I was used to, because our journey was far from over.

When Jude was finally scheduled for a g-tube surgery,

one of the last requirements before going home, we genuinely believed we were nearing the end of the tunnel. It was considered a routine surgery, expected to simplify feeding and provide greater convenience at home, with minimal complications. To me, it symbolized freedom. It was freedom from the hospital, freedom from a stressful nasal feeding tube, and freedom to possibly consolidate Jude's food intake in the future.

After his surgery, Jude spent 24 hours in the PICU to recover. Our nurse hooked up Jude's feeding pump to his g-tube and everything functioned properly. There were no issues, and Jack and I were in a state of bliss. For a moment, we had forgotten the heaviness of medical complications and unmet hopes.

Thanks to morphine, Jude didn't appear to be in pain; he was peacefully resting as his body recovered. We only needed to spend one night in the PICU before we could return to the discharge floor. We felt we were on the verge of finally going home. But we weren't.

Upon returning to the discharge floor, the vomiting started. Jude's stomach began rejecting everything we put into his g-tube, from milk to medication. We tried giving him breaks, changing the fortification, letting air escape his stomach through the g-tube in a process called "venting" — nothing worked. No matter what we did, even if we only gave Jude 5 mL of milk, he immediately spit it up. Eventually, our medical team had no choice but to insert an IV line to provide Jude with essential fluids to keep him hydrated. Once again, we had to watch helplessly as Jude's weight plummeted because it became impossible to feed him.

No one understood what was going on with Jude, especially because he hadn't shown any red flags during the first 24 hours after surgery. We consulted multiple doctors and surgeons, even requesting a fluoroscopy to ensure the tube placement and check for any intestinal blockages, but as usual, all tests came back normal. There was no logical explanation for this adverse reaction to a procedure that was typically successful. We even fed Jude from his nasal feeding tube straight into his stomach for weeks prior to the surgery to prepare his stomach to digest milk again. I was deeply frustrated. This surgery was supposed to be our golden ticket home. I felt like I had been stranded out at sea and finally found a radio, only for it to slip out of my hands and sink beneath the dark waves. The recovery was obviously futile, but there was nothing else to do but try and retrieve what had been lost.

After several days of uncertainty, our attending doctor, whom we had grown fond of, visited us early one morning before rounds. He walked in and leaned over Jude's bed, studying him for a few minutes before meeting our gaze on the other side of the bed railing. After a moment of silence, he admitted that he simply had no idea what was wrong with Jude. He had exhausted every test and explored every avenue, but could not find any clues. In the hundreds upon hundreds of children he had seen receive a g-tube, Jude was the only patient he had that responded this way. His best hypothesis was that Jude's central and parasympathetic nervous systems were both highly sensitive and clearly affected by his lack of oxygen during his initial cardiac arrest. Theoretically, the surgical manipulation of his gut could have "stunned" his intestines, causing them to become unresponsive. Food moves through your gastrointestinal tract by a process called peristalsis, but for Jude, it was almost as if his intestines turned off completely. The only course of action was to wait and hope that, with time, the peristaltic movement of his bowels would normalize.

Jude's entire journey was permeated with ambiguity and confusion. It was never comfortable to receive, but probably just as uncomfortable to give as a doctor. They wanted to make sense of things, to offer treatment options, and yet, they often found themselves apologizing for their inability to provide anything other than a space for us to wait in.

I sat back on the hospital bench and stared at the wall that held Jude's whiteboard for his "goal of the day." It had reverted back to an empty space. The goal of the day had been empty more often than not. Sometimes, all it read was "feed." Now, it couldn't even say that. It also had a space for the estimated discharge day, but nothing was ever written in that box.

Above the board of useless prompts hung the universal pain assessment scale from 1 to 10. I wiped my tears away as I mentally circled 10: hurts as much as possible.

5

Where They Leave You

"For these things I weep; My eyes run down with water; Because far from me is a comforter, One who restores my soul."
- Lamentations 1:16 (NASB)

The day I discovered I was pregnant with Jude, even though I was filled with excitement, I sat on my bed and cried for half an hour. Jack and I were eager to embrace this new chapter, but I had become overwhelmed by the idea of letting go of the life I had known. I realized that my life, as I knew it, was forever changed. I was thrilled to have the privilege of starting a family, but simultaneously, I mourned the life around me that I knew would gradually peel away like old paint from the walls.

I had an indescribable fear that stepping into motherhood would isolate me from the world, my friends, and even my husband. I couldn't shake this feeling that I would be alone, and I prayed against stepping into a season of isolation, a prayer that I can only imagine created quite an awkward silence in the heavenly realm. I was about to experience the single most isolating event in my entire life when Jude's heart stopped and I spent the better part of a year in the hospital. The isolation grew even more profound when I realized I would be going home with a baby who had acquired disabilities that no one could have forewarned me of. Ultimately, I had to walk through the darkest and most isolating valley of them all: the loss of a child. I had been concerned about stepping into motherhood before most of the women in my life, but I had an entirely deeper form of exile waiting before me.

After Jude's problematic g-tube surgery, feeding him became a trial-and-error process for several days. To be honest, Jude's GI tract was simply never the same after surgery, and it frustrated me that no one had really discussed the possibility of that with us, no matter how unlikely. I knew that I would have consented to the surgery regardless, as he needed to eat, and his nasal feeding tubes were too easily dislodged. He had also become mobile enough in his hands to easily rip out his nasal feeding tubes, unaware of the unfortunate series of events that would have to unfold if he did, from 40 minutes of needle pricks to days without nutrition as we waited for an opening in the schedule to replace the tube.

A week passed of Jude being sustained on fluids alone. He reverted to a state of misery, crying most waking hours. He lost over a pound of weight. A pound we worked so hard for him to gain, lost in a matter of days. We slowly weaned Jude back on milk, but he needed the help of suppositories to keep things moving in his intestines. To make matters worse, Jude was experiencing significant respiratory distress, and we couldn't determine if it was due to the vomiting or a separate issue. Every time he vomited, we lived in constant fear that it would end up in his lungs, potentially causing an infection. As it turned out, one of Jude's stitches on his stomach had become infected, and they needed to start him on antibiotics immediately. If any momentum had survived, this surely squashed it. We had to give Jude another 10 days to fight off the infection before we could move forward with anything else.

As soon as his infection cleared, we coordinated with our medical team to schedule a sleep study for Jude. They set it for Sunday night, September 18. At this point, we were making slight progress with Jude's g-tube feeds, but he could only tolerate continuous, 24/7 feedings in small increments — no bolus feedings. If this was enough to get us home, it was enough for me. I had learned to take what I could get.

Typically, medical staff don't discharge patients on continuous feeds and would prefer some level of consolidation, but after enduring countless setbacks, I made it clear that I would not stay in the hospital for weeks on end solely to wait for Jude's feedings to consolidate. That goal could theoretically take weeks to months and was something we could achieve at home. The longer Jude was in the hospital, the more likely it was he would get an infection that required him to stay in the hospital. They were reluctant, but given we had lived in CHLA for over 100 days at this point, I think they understood my frustration. We had literally been there longer than some of our resident doctors had worked there.

Thankfully, Jude's infection cleared up in time for his scheduled sleep study, and Jack and I waited anxiously after he went to sleep to ensure everything appeared okay before returning to the Ronald McDonald House for the night. I was so relieved he had secured the sleep study spot. They were challenging to schedule, and given the pattern of the past few months, I clung to any good news with white knuckles because it was all too often snatched away from me at the last minute. Everything seemed to be aligning for us to finally go home, so I thought I could lay my head down to sleep that night. My mistake.

I awoke to my phone ringing at 6 a.m., jolting me out of a deep sleep. My heart raced immediately, and I knew even before answering that the call was from CHLA.

I always hoped that it was something small, like asking if I could bring more breast milk to the hospital, but I knew it was something bad — bad enough that they couldn't wait one hour for us to arrive at the hospital as we always did.

"Hello?"

It was our resident doctor, Sam, who had been working with us for several weeks. The first thing he told me was that everything was fine, and Jude was okay, which essentially translated to everything was not fine, and Jude was not okay, but he was technically alive.

Sam informed me that Jude had coded early that morning, indicating respiratory or cardiac arrest. They didn't know why. His oxygen levels had dropped to the 60s, the lowest we had ever seen. For reference, your oxygen saturation should ideally be at 100, or at least above 95. Anything below 92 is considered hypoxic, meaning your body doesn't have sufficient oxygen to maintain homeostasis. If a pulse oximeter picks up SpO2 under 92, alarms will go off. As the numbers fall, the alarm gets increasingly louder, faster, and begins blinking yellow, and then red. I'll probably remember that sound for the rest of my life.

Jack and I rushed to the hospital, which was only a couple blocks from the Ronald McDonald House. Upon arrival, they informed us that Jude's oxygen had dropped and then spontaneously returned to normal. They conducted chest x-rays and a blood test, ruling out infection. We were immensely grateful for this because if Jude had an infection, it would have meant another couple of weeks in the hospital and the invalidation of the sleep study. The medical team couldn't find any reason for Jude's oxygen drop and concluded it was a "BRUE": a brief resolved unexplained event. It's a lovely acronym medical staff use to give "I have no idea why this happened" a proper sounding diagnosis.

Jude was in bad shape, but bad shape was his baseline,

unfortunately. We had no choice but to move forward. After allowing Jude a few days to rest, we planned for his potential discharge on September 22, which also happened to be the day Jude turned four months old. The anticipation of reaching the end of our journey, with a scheduled discharge date in sight, was a mix of emotions — excitement and heaviness intertwined. But, the morning of September 22, Jude experienced another episode and his SpO2 dropped to the 60s, requiring a call to the rapid response team and as much oxygen support as they could give outside of an ICU. Our medical team grew increasingly concerned and ordered additional x-rays, which revealed that Jude's atelectasis had worsened, resulting in further lung collapse. They told us it went without saying, but Jude would obviously not be discharging today.

In the following hours, Jude developed a fever, and our medical team decided to initiate treatment for another lung infection. Once again, the ground seemed to shift beneath us. These repeated traumatic events made it nearly impossible for us to feel anything but constant distress. The inside of my mind became a hostile environment, one that couldn't support the growth of anything hopeful. The way our discharge date dangled in front of my exhausted, bloodshot eyes affected my psyche in ways probably buried deep within my subconscious. For months on end, we had been told by our medical team that Jude only needed a few more things to get done, but his instability and misfortune had caused them to push it back "a couple weeks more" too many times.

Each floor had a different theme, and the discharge floor was desert-themed. Bright and early every morning, I trudged through the same hallways to make it to morning rounds. I told myself to make it just one more day, and then another. I was in a marathon, but I didn't know how many miles were left. I didn't know if I was almost at the finish line or if I wasn't even halfway there. What I did know was that there was no way I could make it if I focused on anything other than the next step in front of me.

I wore oversized t-shirts and leggings, probably the same ones I slept in. My hair wasn't brushed and I hadn't slept for more than a couple hours at a time in months. I would push past the large crowds of doctors and nurses who were all arriving at the hospital at the same time. They were so put together, not a hair out of place. They all piled into the hospital halls in scrubs and white coats, swiftly walking next to their friends whom they chatted with loudly. The sound of life roared all around me. This was their place of work but it was my place of exile.

In the ancient Hebrew mind, a circle represented "order" because order was seen as the cyclical process of life and death, otherwise seen as renewal and destruction. The Hebrew people viewed wilderness as a place of order, in contrast to cities which would have been seen as a place of chaos. The word "wilderness" or "desert" in Hebrew is *midbar*, and it shows up 272 times in the Bible. The root word for *midbar* is *devar*, which means "word" or "to speak." One of the pictographs for the root word *devar* illustrates a house or a womb, which tells us the wilderness can also be a place of compassion and rebirth. The wilderness is a recurring theme in the Bible, as it follows stories of Abraham, David, the Israelites, and even Jesus in exile. It suggests that humanity itself is in a form of exile, separated from God and operating under broken systems.

I share this little etymological lesson with you because the wilderness was seen by the ancient Israelites as a place where you can go to hear the word of God. It's interesting that a dry, desolate place where crops cannot grow is where God leads us to hear his word, a place to find order and compassion. God did not take the Israelites straight to the

Promised Land from Egypt, he took his people on a journey to wander the desert for 40 years. When Jesus found himself in the wilderness, it tells us the Spirit is the one who led him there. This place of loneliness, isolation, and hopelessness is actually a place God takes us to speak to us.

If you've ever been in the middle of the desert, it's hard not to become overwhelmed or even frightened by how removed you are, not just from civilization, but from life itself. Barely anything can survive out there. It's entirely counterintuitive that it is chosen as the place where we go to encounter God. The desert is where Jesus was baptized. The desert is where God makes himself known, where we can find a sense of order through the cycle of recreation after destruction. To seek the living water, we go where no other water flows.

As the hospital's elevator doors opened to those desert-themed walls on the discharge floor, I had a revelation that this was our time of isolation. This was our wilderness, and God had led us here. He was with us, even while we were crawling on our hands and knees, reaching out desperately to every mirage, only for it to dissipate into the sand the closer we got.

Eventually, I grabbed hold of something real. After Jude had finished his antibiotic treatment, September 29 was set as his official discharge date. Jude could barely tolerate being fed and his lungs were in extraordinarily poor health, but there was no solution anyone could offer. Void of answers, our team decided to start the process of sending us home. A medical equipment company sent a respiratory therapist named Alex to our hospital room to deliver everything we needed to care for Jude on our own. Jack and I eagerly awaited his arrival, anticipating the beginning of Jude's homecoming.

Alex arrived at our hospital room around 8 p.m.

He introduced himself and started unloading boxes of equipment from a dolly. As Alex rolled the dolly out of the room to collect more boxes, my face fell. I realized that this was only a fraction of Jude's required equipment. My initial excitement gave way to disbelief as I watched our hospital room become buried under a mountain of cardboard. Alex continued to roll the dolly out of the room and back in to unload more boxes, strategically placing them to clear a pathway on the floor.

As we began unpacking the equipment, I noticed that the at-home devices were bulkier and louder than the ones in the hospital. Alex provided tutorials on how to use and maintain these unfamiliar machines, but darkness crept closer as fear and dread overwhelmed me. I struggled to speak without crying as my gaze fell on these anchors that would be attached to my son, perhaps forever. The oxygen concentrator alone resembled a small dresser, and Jude needed to be connected to it at all times. There was a cold metal medical pole for his feeding pump, a suction machine the size of a car battery that vibrated the floor with its deafening noise, a nebulizer with numerous pieces, masks, adapters, and tubing, and a cough assist machine even larger than the suction machine. I couldn't believe the amount of machinery it took to accomplish what our bodies should just do naturally.

I couldn't fathom where to place it all or how we were expected to integrate it into our lives. How could we ever leave our apartment? Would everything even fit? How do people do this?

I gazed out of the window at the glittering Los Angeles skyline, a backdrop I had grown too familiar with, and I realized — people don't do this.

I remembered.

I remembered that this is our life now, but for most

people, it's not. It's a system created by those who have never had to use it. It's delivered by people like Alex who are removed from it, just trying to complete their last call of the night so they can go home to their own families. Even though we were in one of the country's largest children's hospitals, surrounded by staff immersed in a medical environment of chronic illness, disability and trauma...I still felt completely alone. Few people truly understood this. They sell it, they explain it, they work with it, but at the end of the day, it isn't their child. It isn't their life. They don't need to worry about whether their apartment is accessible or whether the seven machines their child was tethered to would fit in their Toyota Corolla. They don't need to navigate through hundreds of hospital bills, make calls to insurance companies, apply for Medi-Cal, and acquaint themselves with countless state programs and county services, each one more confusing than the last. No, I was the one who had to dive headfirst into this new life, and as I looked around, I realized that everyone else stood silently at the edge of the pool. Each resident, doctor, respiratory therapist, paramedic, nurse, friend, and family member — every one of their faces mirrored in the icy blue water, waiting for me to jump. We would be involuntarily thrown into the deep end. There was no helicopter coming to airlift us out. We had to learn how to swim.

This is where they leave you.

This is where you have to go alone.

———

On September 29, after 120 days in the hospital, Jude was discharged from CHLA. The manager of the discharge floor escorted us out of the hospital herself when our nurse announced that Jude was ready to go. Jude was on a first-name basis with hospital staff, partly because he had become one of their longest and most demanding patients, but also because many of the nurses said they had never had a "Jude" before, so he was easy to remember. He became a minor celebrity thanks to his incessant alarms, code blues, and visits from the rapid response team. Even though Jude was identified as a patient with complex needs, he was also identified as the boy who was never without his mother or father, and that stood as my greatest accomplishment. I loved that there were notes in his chart informing staff that his parents were "very involved and understanding." I loved that our team of doctors and residents came to expect us each time they entered the room, knowing they wouldn't be leaving without answering a few questions. I even loved that we would get in trouble for operating all of Jude's equipment. Jude went through a hell I couldn't stop, but I could leave knowing I never let him go through it alone.

When we walked out the hospital's large double doors, sunlight greeted us with an intensity I wasn't expecting for late afternoon. Jude thrashed his head from side to side, attempting to avoid this hot, intrusive light, a sensation he could probably only compare to the doctor's flashlights when checking his pupil response.

As you might assume, no one gives you a special needs stroller for your newly arriving bundle of joy at your baby shower. Jude's stroller overflowed with medical supplies and machines as we rolled our oxygen tanks behind ourselves. His large pulse oximeter glared ominously at us, my eyes anxiously glancing at it every few seconds. When Jack drove our car up, I placed Jude into the car seat I never thought I would see him in again. I took a deep breath, exhaling gratitude that God had given him back to me. We struggled to fit all the equipment into our small car and I sat squeezed in the back with Jude, medical supplies piled to the roof on every side of me. Still, I knew nothing would be as suffocating and no burden would be as heavy as Jude's absence if he were not sitting in that car seat next to me.

We embarked on the long drive back home, our first time outside in several months. Driving in a car again, watching the hills pass by on the freeway, I felt like a released prisoner reentering society. We were different people now. Memories of doctors telling me to seek professional help came back to mind. I remembered the caring eyes locked on mine, hands placed on my shoulder, soft but firm voices telling me I have endured severe trauma. I didn't know what to do with this juxtaposition between worlds. The external world hadn't changed a bit but my internal world was something completely different. Something I couldn't even yet identify amidst the rubble. For someone who had advocated so strongly to leave the hospital, the terror of no longer being in one quickly set in. Jude's life was anything but stable, but we didn't see any other choice.

The sunset flooded through our windows with a deep orange hue. It was beautiful, and Jude was content, but something inside me was broken and I feared it wasn't going to turn back on.

Funny how feelings linger, even if we pay them no mind. Have you ever felt dreadful over something all day, but then a moment comes, perhaps you get distracted, and you realize that you have forgotten to think about it? Soon afterward, the dread creeps back, but you can't remember why. Your mind seeks to find the reason for it so you can carry on with your worry, but you seem to have lost your way. Even if the reason has been misplaced, the dread remains. Even if the mind has forgotten, the body remembers. Though we were headed home, it didn't feel that way, and I couldn't place why.

In the car, I held tightly onto Jude's strict schedule. I received a hard copy from our nurse before we left the discharge floor. She said she gave a printout of schedules for the more "medically complex" children. Every hour was meticulously planned. I still had to pump milk every couple hours for Jude, carefully package it, label it, and keep it on ice.

With the high demands of pumping, some offered the option of switching Jude to formula. As time consuming, sleep depriving and stressful as pumping was, I held onto it the same way I did that first night in the PICU when our nurse asked me if I would like to use their breast pump. Among his life of medications and artificially lit hospital rooms, breast milk was the only natural thing left in Jude's life.

Jude's schedule also included numerous nebulized treatments, administered every four hours around the clock. Each nebulizer session took about an hour to complete. He was connected to oxygen tanks in the car and needed regular chest physiotherapy, ideally before and after each nebulized treatment for around fifteen minutes or so. Additionally, Jude needed at least one medication every couple of hours, and his feeding pump was continuous, with the milk fortified to specific requirements depending on the volume. Breast milk could only be left out for a few hours before it had to be replaced with fresh milk. Ideally, a new feeding bag should be used, but if not, the used one had to be rinsed and cleaned. Jude also required frequent suctioning, every 30-45 seconds, as saliva and mucus accumulated in his nose and mouth. These tasks were not easy to accommodate while on the road.

To add to our stress, we were also on a time crunch. We didn't receive every one of Jude's medications at CHLA and some needed to be picked up at our local pharmacy, which closed at 9 p.m.

We arrived home just around that time, exhausted. We unpacked the car in the darkness and returned to our apartment. As I watched Jack's silhouette fumble with the keys to unlock the door, I couldn't help but feel we were breaking and entering into a home that was no longer ours. When we walked inside, I didn't get any warm, fuzzy welcoming feeling. Despite returning home, I could have burst into tears any moment. Our apartment was the most depressing time capsule, perfectly preserving the night we left it. Each detail took us back in time to what life was before all this happened. This home had only known joy, but now, we were returning four months later with our child on life support.

Once we tried to settle in, our living room became overwhelmed by medical equipment and the necessities we had relied on for the past four months. It no longer resembled a home. It took every ounce of strength within my exhausted heart not to cry, but Jude went right ahead. We quickly realized we were behind on Jude's treatments and medications, because that's what happened any time we were preoccupied with anything else for longer than an hour. I was due to pump again, we hadn't eaten all day, and it was getting late. Jack still needed to pick up the medications before the pharmacies closed, and with tensions running high, we found ourselves snapping at each other while Jude screamed in our living room.

To keep things interesting, there has to be some kind of technical difficulties. Our pulse oximeter, which Jude always needed to be connected to, inconveniently malfunctioned. If the wire wasn't positioned just right, Jude's vitals either read incorrectly or disappeared entirely. With a critically ill and unstable child, you can imagine the immense stress that comes from not knowing if their oxygen level is at 77 or 97. Beads of sweat ran down our faces as we both knelt on the floor, wrestling over the wires. It was a maddening struggle until we realized the issue lay with the machine itself, which only added to our frustration.

Moments later, as we dug through our bags, we found that no one provided us the right syringes that adapted to Jude's g-tube. As a result, we couldn't even administer his medication. Jack rushed out to swing by the almost closed pharmacy and tirelessly called multiple hospitals in search of the necessary syringes. Meanwhile, I had to simultaneously administer Jude's nebulized treatment while also pumping more breast milk. His heart rate climbed as I sat helplessly fumbling about with no available hands under a dim ceiling light. The cacophony of the suction machine and nebulizer reverberated through our cramped apartment like an insistent lawnmower as Jude screamed on my lap. Jack's absence stretched on for what felt like an eternity. We still hadn't eaten, and when Jack finally returned, we fought about who could go to grab food. It hadn't even been a couple hours and our home had already become a place we needed to escape from. Ultimately, we deemed it fair that I get to take on the next errand that allowed a break from the misery.

I will never forget that night. It stands as one of the most harrowing nights of my entire life, second only to the day Jude initially suffered his cardiac arrest and the day he ultimately passed away. As I got into the car, my suppressed sadness began to rise in me like nausea. Tears streamed down my face uncontrollably as my brain struggled to remember how to operate a car. I peeled out of the silent parking lot. My sobs resonated between the streetlights and the shadows, my hands pounding the steering wheel in frustration as the sadness expelled from my body in the form of a guttural scream.

All this time I had been fighting for us to go home and I never considered the fact that nothing about home still existed. The hospital had felt like prison and now our home did too. I crumbled under the hopeless realization that there would never be an escape. Jude's life was hanging in the balance minute by minute, dependent on equipment he would be tied to in an apartment we could never leave, with disabilities that could be terribly severe.

As I drove past familiar parks, distant memories floated through the rear view mirror, offering a glimpse of a happier, more carefree time. I was pregnant and laughing, begging Jack to stop taking photos of me. Jack and I were excitedly poking at Jude in my belly, eagerly anticipating the places we couldn't wait to show him. But now, the weight of grief pressed down on me like an anvil, its intensity almost unbearable. I struggled to regain my composure before returning to the apartment, where the demands of caring for Jude took precedence for the next couple hours. I set the food I had picked up on the counter, where it grew cold and remained untouched.

Jude eventually succumbed to exhaustion and fell asleep. Jack helped me take all his equipment upstairs as I laid him in his bassinet for the first time in four months. A bassinet that would not have recognized him. As I stared at the mess of our surroundings, the reminders from our past life stood starkly against the tragedy of our current reality. I couldn't help but place my hand over my mouth, trying to stifle my sadness as the tears silently streamed down my face. I didn't understand how we were going to move on from this point. How were we going to live like this? How were either of us ever supposed to work? How were we supposed to prepare meals? To grocery shop? The sheer amount of equipment tethered to Jude required two people just to move him from one place to another. It all felt impossible.

That night, I managed maybe two hours of sleep. That was all that was allotted between Jude's schedule and my pumping, not to mention his broken pulse oximeter that literally alarmed every 10 minutes (an alarm that is designed to wake you up with a life-threatening emergency, so I'll let you imagine what it sounds like). It felt as though we had been home for years, and it had only been a couple days. Jude's frequent vomiting heightened our anxiety. Our suction machine was used so frequently that we just left it on so it was immediately available to prevent aspiration. It roared next to us wherever we went, day and night, robbing us of experiencing even one peaceful, quiet moment.

Before the end of our second day home, Jude vomited every single time I turned on his feeding pump. The one thing I managed to get done was collect all of our untouched bottles we got from our baby shower and give them away to a swap shop our complex had down the block. I almost surrendered them angrily, throwing the box up on a shelf. We couldn't use these bottles, but lots of other parents who had no idea how lucky they were could. I knew Jude had completely surpassed his window to ever learn to drink milk again. Maybe one day we could teach him to eat solids, but it wouldn't be anytime soon.

At home, Jude was miserable, crying constantly, and we couldn't figure out how to help him, especially with our suboptimal medical equipment. His pulse oximeter was showing that he was desatting after he vomited for the fifth time, and we did everything we could to reposition the wire to ensure it was reading correctly.

It was.

Jude was desatting, and his oxygen was only dropping further. In a panic, Jack and I surrounded him, suctioning him, patting his back, giving him all the oxygen we had, but we couldn't get his oxygen levels to rise. We called the 24/7 line at CHLA to talk to a pulmonologist who recommended we go to the nearest emergency room. We were running on no sleep or food and were doing our best to gather all of

Jude's things before frantically driving him to the ER.

In the backseat, I shouted the dropping SpO2 numbers at Jack as he swerved through traffic, praying Jude stayed alive. We finally got to the ER and a nurse was already outside waiting to usher us in. They immediately hooked Jude up to a higher oxygen flow and began deep suctioning him to clear his airways. Jude began vomiting all of his gastric contents as a result of the catheters getting pushed down his throat. His vomit was dark brown, meaning he had some kind of internal bleeding happening.

After taking a chest x-ray, I saw the respiratory therapist outside the ER room staring at the screen when the results came up. Her face became twisted with worry as she waved me over. I ran to her side and saw Jude's typical x-ray, a collapsed lung. I tried to explain to her that this is always what Jude's lungs looked like and she nodded slowly, failing at her attempt to present a calm face so as to not panic me further. Jude had some of the worst x-rays they had ever seen, so I'm sure she considered me crazy when I said he essentially operates with just one (poorly functioning) lung.

Shortly after those x-rays, they swiftly admitted us to PICU, the very same one Jude had been admitted to back in June following his cardiac arrest. In some ways, it triggered difficult memories, but given the intense isolation that Jack and I had been grappling with, it weirdly offered a degree of comfort. While I couldn't help but feel disappointed about returning to an ICU less than 48 hours after leaving CHLA, I also felt a profound sense of relief. The past couple days at home made it apparent that Jude required an intensive hospital environment to survive. He needed high flow oxygen, IV fluids when he wasn't tolerating milk (which was almost constantly now), and medication available on a moment's notice. Though the hospital had never been able to offer us solutions, they could still provide more for Jude's instability than we realistically could at home.

In the PICU, Jude was immediately put on a high-flow machine capable of delivering 100% oxygen. For reference, you and I only breathe around 21% oxygen. It gave Jude a break from his labored breathing. I wondered if he felt more comfortable in this familiar space. I both despised and was relieved by the fact that he probably did.

While Jude rested in bed, Dr. M, the intensivist who had initially stabilized Jude on the night of his cardiac arrest, burst into our hospital room. His attention was immediately drawn to Jude, and he marveled as he observed Jude's eyes tracking his movements across the room. With an exuberant laugh, he raised Jude into the air and embraced him tightly, declaring Jude to be a miracle. It was evident he was not expecting Jude to survive, let alone seem so neurologically intact.

Dr. M expressed his gratitude that we were once again part of "this community," and those words felt like a comforting embrace, welcoming us back from the cold and unforgiving wilderness. We were undeniably drowning, and being at the hospital finally gave us a moment to catch our breath. We had access to high-quality equipment and the incessant alarms that haunted us at home were no longer a constant reminder of our struggle to keep afloat.

A nurse walked into the room and handed me a cup of water and a menu of food I could order for tomorrow's breakfast. I stared at the condensation rolling down the cup for a moment before drinking the entire thing. I hadn't eaten or had more than a sip or two of water in days. All I had wanted was to leave the hospital and go home, but now, the hospital felt more like home. It was the only place others could offer me a seat and a glass of water and a warm blanket. It was the only place people could do something other than gaze out their telescopes at my disastrous storm.

I may not like it, but it was the life we had, and I could not exchange it for the life that no longer existed. Through the gift of medical professionals, God had provided for me, even though my prayers came out as screams and frustrated fists pounding against the steering wheel.

In our smaller local hospital, everything was more personal. We were familiar with all the doctors and staff because there was just one team. In LA, we had a new team every week, and seeing familiar faces was a rarity. After closely monitoring Jude's vitals long enough to feel assured that he was stable, I leaned back in the familiar hospital chair and closed my eyes. I wasn't fighting to breathe for Jude. I wasn't rushing him to an ER. I wasn't trying to comfort him from the pain I could not stop. For that fleeting moment, however brief, I found myself able to appreciate the fact that my son was in the hospital. It was the first time I felt I could rest.

Our home had become uninhabitable. The hospital had become a Petri dish of sorts for us to gather what we needed to live another day. Yes, it was an artificial sanctuary, but a sanctuary nonetheless.

6

The Way of Paradoxes

"For now we see in a mirror dimly, but then face to face. Now I know in part; then I shall know fully, even as I have been fully known."
- 1 Cor. 13:12 (ESV)

"This is not your schedule," Dr. M exclaimed in disbelief as he examined Jude's 24-hour care sheet that I handed to him. "You're getting up at midnight, at 3 a.m., at 4 a.m.?"

I nodded quietly, noting that he wasn't even considering the fact that I was also pumping, which required me to be up every two hours for around thirty minutes.

"This is inhumane," Dr. M said, shaking his head in disapproval before handing the schedule back to me. "We need to change this."

Quickly, Jack and I discovered that the staff at our local hospital's PICU did not approve of what CHLA had sent us home with. They believed that Jude's schedule was far beyond what we could reasonably manage, and it was abundantly clear that we needed professional help, which should have been arranged before we left the hospital. In other words, Jude required home nursing.

After reviewing Jude's chest x-rays, the medical staff didn't believe he had a lung infection, but rather pneumonitis — an inflammation of the lungs due to aspiration. They thought he needed time to heal, but in the interim, we had to find a better solution for his feeding tube problems. Many doctors tend to overlook food intolerance issues related to feeding tubes so long as the child is gaining weight. But Jude couldn't protect his airway, so we were seriously concerned about frequent vomiting. We couldn't rush him to the ER every time he aspirated. Given that Jude had shown signs of dried blood in his vomit during his emergency room visit, there were concerns that he might have ulcers. Blood alone can be very irritating to the stomach, so there was also the possibility that the blood was the cause of his vomiting.

The plan was to keep Jude on an IV to let both his respiratory system and his stomach recover in the PICU. Afterward, we could transfer him to the pediatric wing down the hall to address any feeding tolerance issues. There, we would work with GI specialists.

Despite the seemingly straightforward plan and the optimism of Dr. M, Jack and I were all too familiar with life in the hospital by this point. We understood that we should brace ourselves for at least a few more weeks here. We saw this as an opportunity not only to sort out home nursing but also to decide whether we should relocate within our apartment complex to better accommodate Jude's needs.

Our current place was a small, two-story apartment with a narrow and steep staircase, which made moving Jude and his equipment quite challenging and required two people at all times. We discussed the possibility of moving to one of the other apartments in the complex, a single-story unit with additional storage space for all of Jude's equipment. We needed to build a brand new life, one capable of supporting Jude.

Initially, everything appeared to be going according to plan when we successfully weaned Jude off his high-flow oxygen in just one week and put him back on a low-flow nasal cannula. Doctors theorized that the bleeding in his stomach likely resulted from irritation caused by the g-tube balloon rubbing against the stomach wall, so we introduced another medication into Jude's schedule to coat his stomach and alleviate any discomfort.

With Jude on lower respiratory support, we were able to transfer him out of the PICU and into the pediatric wing after just one week.

The next day, Jude's oxygen dropped to the 70s. Jack and I watched the familiar chaos unfold as nurses and doctors rushed in to attempt to get Jude's oxygen back up. Despite their attempts, the situation resolved on its own.

Another chest x-ray unsurprisingly revealed the collapse of Jude's entire right lung. Everyone was appalled Jude's lungs were still presenting so poorly and wanted to treat him for a lung infection. Even before they mentioned it, I jumped to inform them about Jude's severely limited vein access. Not only was he a baby with small veins, but repeated IV therapy can damage veins, rendering them useless until they heal. We couldn't help but envy CHLA's IV team which used ultrasound machines to find optimal veins for babies quickly. The IV team got a better look at which veins were viable before they began poking around, which resulted in a lot less unnecessary pain for Jude. They typically found a vein within 10 or 15 minutes. Unfortunately, our smaller hospital lacked such resources. Ultrasound-guided IV teams were primarily assigned to the ER and the NICU, and they were called in only after numerous failed attempts by other nurses. I tried to explain that Jude had no more veins left to use, but I still had to hold him down for 30 minutes while nurses jabbed needles into his skin.

Pain stretches every moment into a small eternity. Jude screamed powerlessly as they inserted and removed various devices from his tiny body. He had reached an age where he recognized me and his blue eyes would plead for help. My own eyes would well up with tears as I held him down, unable to provide the comfort I longed to give. At times, I would turn my head away, allowing the tears to cascade down my cheeks and onto the floor, prompting the medical team to ask if I needed a break. Psychologically, I have found it is difficult for the mind to make sense of an experience that would be deemed abuse if it were not placed in a medical context.

Eventually they called in the IV team, who spent another 45 minutes trying to find a vein. After multiple failed attempts and lots of bruising, it was decided that we needed to send Jude to interventional radiology to place a central line in his jugular vein. This line would later cause Jude a blood infection which needed to be immediately treated with antibiotics since the jugular vein drains directly into the right atrium of the heart. Soon after treating the infection, the central line would then move halfway out of Jude's neck, requiring an emergency removal. At that point, I once again found myself restraining Jude for 20 minutes as they fished this line that was sutured in yet protruding out of his neck. This procedure had left several permanent scars on Jude's neck that sometimes garnered questions from people who spotted it, curious to know what had happened to him.

Nothing triggered a visceral reaction out of me quite like facilitating the suffering of my child, even if it was for his ultimate good. I couldn't help but draw parallels between myself and Jude as both of us were looking above to plead to our higher powers to please do something. I was suffering, and I knew full well God had the ability to stop it, yet he chose not to. In fact, it felt as though he was the one holding me there.

Though it may seem so, God is not orchestrating cruel twists of fate for us. We are all just struggling to live in a world that is mercilessly chaotic and unjust, much of which is fueled by our own greed and selfish desires. We must also continue the frustrating fight of holding these painful truths in light of a God who allows them, a God who witnesses every last tear fall from our eyes.

It occurred to me how easily Jude could misinterpret my actions in those moments. He might conclude that I didn't love him, that he held no value in my eyes, or even question my identity as his mother because of the suffering he endured. I began to grasp that these seemingly contradictory statements could coexist:

God loves you.

God is all-powerful.

God's will is not for you to suffer.

This was a paradox I could identify in my own relationship with my son. I loved Jude immensely and wished nothing more than to take away his pain. It was also true that I did, technically, have the power to stop his suffering. Each painful procedure required my consent, and more often than not, I was the one physically restraining him. I had all the power to let go. In fact, I had all the power to pick up my baby, wrap him in a blanket, curse out the medical staff, and take him home.

And nothing was more true than this: that was also my will. My will was to bring him home. My will was to stop the pain. My will was to cradle him in my arms, dry his tears, and assure him that everything would be alright. How could all of these seemingly conflicting realities coexist?

If Jude's will was for the pain to stop and to go home, and my will mirrored his, and I was the one compelling him to endure suffering — how could he equate this with love?

I suppose I would hope he would consider another variable: perhaps, there's more than meets the eye. Perhaps, there's something he doesn't understand, a greater good he doesn't see. As much as I hate his pain, my perspective afforded me the ability to discern when suffering is worth its product.

Furthermore, my perspective allowed me to evaluate whether the "good thing" he yearned for was truly the best thing for him. A great deal of parenthood involves the ongoing effort to convey to children that the alluring, shiny thing they are grasping at isn't exactly what they imagine it to be. They confuse grenades for gemstones.

Daily, I wrestled with the urge to push everyone aside, end Jude's suffering, and take him home — but what would that truly look like in reality? He would slowly succumb to a blood infection due to the lack of antibiotics. He would waste away from malnutrition because I wouldn't be able to feed him. He might choke on his own saliva or suffocate from collapsed lungs if I couldn't offer the respiratory support he required.

Of course, Jude didn't know any of that, because his vision was obscured the same way yours and mine is. Knowledge eludes us. The suffering we endure is overwhelming and the burdens we carry are substantial. And yet, we focus our eyes on the one who assures us of his promise of presence. He is the one who is holding our hand through it all, with tears filling his eyes as he whispers,

I know. I wish it were not so. I'm going to make it better soon. Please trust me.

—

In the pediatric wing, we were stuck in an endless loop of feeding intolerance, oxygen desats, collapsed lungs, IV placements, antibiotics, repeat. The desats became increasingly severe and intense, falling lower than the ones we experienced at CHLA.

Jude endured two consecutive desats, plummeting

as low as 60% SpO2. The attending doctor had only just managed to calm the chaos in our room following Jude's event, spending barely five minutes outside before hurrying back in when alarms started blaring. Jude's oxygen levels fell yet again: 80s, 70s, 60s. The respiratory therapists were deep suctioning him and this frustrated me. Deep suctioning is a profoundly traumatic experience, and it was evident to me that secretions were not obstructing Jude's airway. Yet, we possessed thousands of hours' worth of data gathering, while this team was only now entering the scene. They had to run through protocol before they could realize Jude's issues lied beyond their modus operandi.

As Jude's numbers slowly began to rise on their own, the attending doctor took a moment to catch her breath. She examined Jude, listening intently to his lungs through her stethoscope before turning her attention toward us.

"What diagnosis did they give him again?" she asked.

I paused, remembering the discharge notes I received from CHLA that listed up to twenty different diagnoses for Jude's health issues. It was both a loaded and hollow question. The diagnoses overwhelmed my brain: encephalopathy, excessive oral secretions, spasticity, ineffective airway clearance, central sleep apnea, bulbar dysfunction, nocturnal hypoxemia, sleep-disordered breathing, acute chronic respiratory failure with hypoxemia...the list went on. But none of them offered anything of use.

"Hypoxic ischemic encephalopathy," I said. It means brain damage caused by a lack of oxygen and blood flow, so I figured it would broadly cover everything else.

She furrowed her brow, clearly puzzled. She was a doctor accustomed to working at Seattle Children's Hospital, renowned as one of the nation's top pediatric hospitals.

"You typically diagnose that by MRI, though," she said. "Doesn't he have clear MRIs?"

"Yes," I said, silently welcoming her to our torturous and confounding world.

I realized that every new doctor on the team, whether on the pediatric floor or in the ICU, would need to arrive at their own conclusions about Jude and each unique aspect of his peculiar medical history. I grew impatient as we had to repeat the same process all over again. Almost immediately, the doctors began speculating about seizure activity. Some seizures are known as subclinical, meaning they can only be detected by monitoring brain activity since there are no visible symptoms. It had been months since we had given Jude an EEG, but this hospital still hadn't received any of Jude's medical history from CHLA, and they insisted on verifying that he wasn't experiencing seizures.

Our attending doctor decided to transfer Jude back to the PICU because he was too unstable to stay in the pediatric wing and they wanted to conduct another 48 hour EEG. These desats Jude was experiencing were not just unpredictable, they were medically puzzling. Jude wasn't turning blue, his breathing wasn't labored, and his heart rate remained normal, yet he was in a critically hypoxic state. It presented a dangerous obstacle in our goal to get Jude home. If he wasn't hooked up to a monitor, you would have no idea how close he was to death. Then, seemingly out of nowhere, he would spontaneously recover. It was almost as if it didn't matter what anyone did or didn't do. On top of this, this new medical team was struggling to grasp at what was left to provide a patient that has already had every conceivable test.

By the end of the second week, we conducted another EEG in the PICU which, once again, indicated normal brain activity. I started to worry that we were essentially restarting. Jude's medical presentation was so complex that I feared we were destined to relive everything all over again. The uneasiness settled deeper in my stomach when people began questioning the details of my pregnancy and delivery.

If they were going to suggest that Jude's issues might be congenital, I felt like screaming. I had to be asked for the millionth time to describe what Jude was like before his cardiac arrest. The subtle implication that perhaps these were problems he had always faced felt borderline insulting. It reached a point where I had to show medical staff videos of 8-day-old Jude coughing and drinking just to demonstrate that he hadn't always been like this.

A few days later, while still in the PICU, Jude experienced yet another desat. Whatever was going on with Jude, it was getting worse. His oxygen went down to 39. Nothing sends chills down your spine like watching your baby's oxygen drop like a rock on a screen while doctors and nurses rush in to bag them. I hated that I had also become all too familiar with it. I hated that I had to say "yes, this is just a thing he does" to a life-threatening emergency situation.

Our team of doctors and our pulmonologist began reaching out to their colleagues and other experts across the country for advice on how to address Jude's condition. Nothing seemed to align with his symptoms and they couldn't identify a root cause or a solution. There were very few medical explanations for such extreme and sudden oxygen desats like the ones Jude was experiencing. His CO_2 levels were normal, ruling out hyperventilation. His EEGs showed no signs of seizures. His heart rate remained steady, dispelling the notion of apnea. His airway wasn't floppy, and his sleep study indicated no obstructive sleep apnea, confirming his airway was clear. His lungs, however, were some of the worst they'd seen. The presentation was particularly confusing because he would have his right lung collapse one day, followed by his left lung collapsing the next. Sometimes, this occurred within the span of a single day, with one lung collapsing right after the other. Ultimately, Dr. M described Jude as an enigma.

By November, Jude had spent one month in our local hospital and was desatting regularly, both while he was awake and while he was asleep. The medical team had finally spent enough time observing Jude to recognize his patterns, however odd they might be. Even so, his x-rays didn't provide any consistent correlations. Even when Jude struggled to breathe, sometimes his lung scans appeared clearer, while at other times, they were completely white.

Despite having only three rotating PICU doctors, none of them seemed to agree with the others. Each had their own theories, each of which Jack and I found unsatisfactory in one way or another. Some days, I overheard hushed conversations in the hallway between the PICU doctors and the pediatric wing doctors. When they didn't notice me approaching, I heard them whispering that they had no idea what to do with Jude. They quickly fell silent when they recognized me walking by. The unspoken tension was seen on the faces of all the medical staff we got to know too well, even the respiratory therapists and nurses had their frustrations with the lack of solutions. Jude's case seemed to be unlike any they had encountered before, leaving them bewildered about how to proceed or formulate a treatment plan. At times, an intensivist and our pulmonologist would retreat to the conference room to discuss Jude's case, their conversations sometimes escalating into heated arguments lasting for half an hour. It had reached a point where the intensivists started seeking our input, asking if we had any recommendations or ideas.

My frustration reached its peak when the legitimate proposed solution was for us to return to CHLA. Our PICU doctors openly admitted they had exhausted their resources and ideas to help Jude. His respiratory status was only getting worse and we couldn't figure out how or why. They suggested returning to a larger hospital like CHLA, which held more medical history and resources for Jude, but that was not an option I was willing to consider. There were no magic solutions at CHLA, no miracle cure for Jude's neurological issues, no untested procedures left to explore, and no specialists who hadn't already extensively reviewed Jude's case. The only proposed solution for a patient with an increasingly unstable respiratory status would be a tracheostomy, which I was not willing to consent to without anyone showing me any evidence it would help. I would not be choosing medical interventions based on the process of elimination.

So much about Jude's confounding story deepened the sense of alienation we were experiencing. We weren't placed in any category and there was no clear path forward. When your child is hospitalized, you want to hear words like "normal" and "routine," not to witness medical staff huddled in quiet conversations and disputes in conference rooms.

Jack and I didn't just feel disconnected from the outside world; we felt disconnected from the ICU itself. It had been months, and there wasn't any specific goal of being there. We had watched other patients cycle in and out while Jude grew older. There wasn't anything we were treating, anything we were recovering, anything we were solving. Jude was growing up in the hospital solely because he couldn't survive anywhere else. I needed to know, realistically, what life would look like if we tried to take Jude home. In a much needed family meeting, our pulmonologist presented three potential options for Jude to go home with:

CPAP. This would be a nasal mask that would be attached to Jude's face, possibly at all times. It could deliver continuous positive airway pressure. This positive pressure was the only thing that appeared to help Jude expand his lungs, but it wasn't a completely sealed system. If Jude ever opened his mouth, the pressure would dissipate, which might render it useless.

High-Flow Oxygen. This is the support Jude was getting in the PICU, but it's not something patients typically go home on. In fact, no one had ever heard of a patient going home on a high-flow machine. It could deliver heated and humidified 100% oxygen at 12 liters per minute. For reference, Jude had left CHLA on 1.5 liters of oxygen.

Tracheostomy. This was back on the table, but our pulmonologist was wrestling with the same risk factors we were about a trach. If we could connect his oxygen support directly to a tracheostomy tube, it would bypass his nose and mouth entirely and provide a closed system for delivering positive pressure. Still, there was no real reason Jude needed an artificial windpipe, and there were no guarantees of improvement. Moreover, it introduced a host of new potential issues for Jude. Given that Jude had a normally structured airway, it seemed excessive to jeopardize his life in such an invasive and life-altering procedure.

After discussion, our preferred choice was to explore the possibility of Jude going home on high-flow oxygen. It had been sustaining him in the hospital with settings that could be adjusted to fairly high levels and it didn't require a mask or life-threatening surgery. However, the high-flow nasal cannula did come with its own set of challenges. It was bulky and had to be securely fastened to prevent it from slipping off Jude's face. Additionally, it consistently sprayed water into his nose (which he hated) because the elevated oxygen flow could irritate his nostrils to the point of bleeding.

Our doctors were skeptical about this option, as none of them had seen it done before. Our pulmonologist researched extensively, but eventually told us there was no available at-home high-flow machine. Insurance was refusing to approve it, but our pulmonologist began to doubt that it could even be a long-term solution the more he observed Jude. Since it was clear Jude's lungs were collapsing, more oxygen would just be masking the problem. The branches throughout Jude's lungs were getting blocked off, preventing air from reaching deep enough into the bronchial tubes. If Jude's lungs couldn't make a proper gas exchange, it wouldn't matter how much oxygen we were giving. He needed positive pressure to force those branches to stay open.

This left us with only one viable option — a CPAP machine. Finding a CPAP mask suitable for an infant proved to be challenging, and I remembered CHLA informing us that they never discharged infants on CPAP. In fact, they never sent infants home if they required more than 2 liters of oxygen. Our pulmonologist was searching for a ventilator and CPAP mask that would be small enough for Jude. In the meantime, we were able to begin weaning Jude off of high-flow. Since he was back on a low-flow nasal cannula, they felt comfortable switching him back over to the pediatric wing.

Jude did not adapt well to the reduced respiratory support. Even though he was could still receive up to four liters of oxygen in the pediatric wing, he started experiencing severe desats within 24 hours. These desats started to occur in clusters and were not so brief anymore, sometimes lasting as long as 30 minutes. The dark storm that had been looming on the horizon for months was now rapidly advancing toward us. Soon, Jude wasn't even fully recovering after his major desats. He would float around in the 80s despite the extra oxygen support.

Adding to our concerns, Jude began developing frequent fevers. He wasn't showing any other signs of infection, so the doctors figured the fevers were due to the atelectasis. His x-rays worsened, revealing that Jude's heart had completely shifted to the opposite side of his chest, and he had a severe tracheal deviation caused by the pressure shift from his collapsed lungs. This only occurs when there is severe asymmetry of intrathoracic pressures. It felt like one issue piled upon another, and then I received the dreaded phone call one night at 2 a.m.

7

Blessings Still Grow on the Valley Floor

"For the sake of my servant Jacob, and Israel my chosen, I call you by your name, I name you, though you do not know me."
- Isaiah 45:4 (NIV)

"Taylor? Jude desat to the 20s. We think he was showing signs of seizure activity. We are admitting him back to the PICU. You should come here now."

I drove through the rain in the middle of the night, struggling to see clearly through my blurred, tear-filled vision. Jude was deteriorating rapidly. There wasn't much further these desats could drop.

Upon arriving at the hospital lobby and waiting to check in with security, my gaze fixated on a large photo hanging on the wall — an enormous, breathtaking panoramic view of Santa Barbara that stretched across the right wall of the hospital entrance. The photograph captured Santa Barbara's quintessential landscape of its mountainous backdrop towering over the sweeping blue coastline that was sprinkled with palm trees.

A memory rushed to mind, instantaneously transporting me to another life I had once lived. I returned to the day I left this very hospital after giving birth to Jude. My nurse was rolling me through the halls in my wheelchair as I held my bundled newborn in a hospital blanket. I didn't know then, but I would soon grow sick at the sight of those hospital blankets. My hair hadn't been washed and was thrown into a greasy mess on the top of my head. My stomach was a mushy bowl of oatmeal. I didn't care a bit.

The hospital's protocol was to keep me and Jude one more night, but I had pushed to get a slightly earlier discharge. Since his birth, I was always fighting to get Jude home.

As we floated down the hall, everyone stopped to stare at us with big smiles, raised eyebrows, and sweet cheers of congratulations. It was like I was walking down the aisle on my wedding day. My nurse and I chatted about how beautiful the paintings of flowers were that spotted the hallways. I had never noticed them before. She rolled me off the elevator and into the breathtaking hospital lobby I had not yet seen, surrounded with floor to ceiling windows. My eyes were drawn to the panoramic photo in the lobby and I felt overwhelmingly blessed.

I thought to myself, how lucky am I to live here? How lucky are we? I clutched Jude tightly, softly assuring him that he was a profoundly blessed baby. My nurse rolled me outside the double doors and we waited for my husband to eagerly pull up in our little Toyota Corolla.

I've often questioned what it means to be blessed. I believed I was right to feel some sort of favor from God when Jude was born healthy and safe. In the Bible, blessings are invariably linked with life. That's why fertility and children are among the first blessings mentioned. However, I've struggled with this concept in light of Jesus' Sermon on the Mount, where he declares that the blessed are the poor, the mourners, and the hungry. I used to find this perplexing — was it more blessed to have health, family, and comfort, or to endure trials and suffering? When life was golden and I held my healthy baby boy, it felt nothing short of natural to feel blessed, to thank God, to regard that moment as a euphoric gift to be cherished. But when my life seemed to descend into chaos, I turned to the Gospel of Matthew and attempted to align my heart with these promises. Jesus declared the broken and sorrowful people as the favored ones. These were the ones whose hearts had a pathway to heaven. *Theirs* is the kingdom of God.

Through this journey, I've come to realize that it's both. As I stared at that vibrant photo in the hospital lobby, traveling back to a moment when everything appeared perfect, it was indeed a blessing. God had surrounded me with life, health, and beauty. All good things come from him, and that moment was nothing short of divine.

Yet, as my feet were planted on the same hospital floor, feeling void of blessing and full of uncertainty, I believe the blessing still remained. Though it was not readily apparent in earthly terms, it is a blessing to be broken because it allows the light to pour in. It compels us to fall to our knees and know our dependence. It grants us a distinct form of spiritual clarity and wisdom. Brokenness, at times, is a different but often more powerful lens than goodness through which to experience God.

I often would reflect on the countless people who reached out to me and shared that they were praying for Jude. His tragic story had touched the hearts of many, and I was deeply humbled to receive messages from people across state lines and even from different countries, all praying for Jude's recovery. Among the most remarkable prayers to me were those from people who openly admitted they were not believers, and they did not pray, but they would pray for Jude with everything they had. I often wondered about their relationship with prayer and what it would mean to them if Jude did not survive.

We tend to perceive God's presence in our lives as manifested solely through a saved life, a healed sickness, a medical miracle exploding onto the scene. While these gifts are undeniably wonderful, I wanted those praying for Jude to understand that God's goodness had already been demonstrated. His work was already unfolding the moment an unbeliever's knees hit the floor. Regardless of whether Jude lived or died, God's love was vividly on display when human beings decided to show compassion for one another.

They were blessed with the ability to view someone through the eyes of God by recognizing the inherent worth of God's creation. That meant shedding tears when a baby was in the hospital. That meant humbling oneself before a God one did not believe in. That meant having the courage to send a message to a friend who you haven't spoken to in over a decade. That meant waking up at 5 a.m. day after day for a 12 hour hospital shift to care for the sick and disabled. I believe that these acts of worship are often fueled by God's spirit more than the average church attendance. They represented sacrifice, mercy, humility, and unwavering commitment.

We are blessed to know truth, and sometimes, truth is most effectively delivered through our experiences of suffering. By crying out to God in hopes of healing an innocent life — my friend, the gift has already been given. Perhaps there wasn't any change in circumstance, but I have faith in the power of prayer to shape our inner worlds. I'm sorry it is not always obvious, but even through a simple prayer, you have carried out God's love. You have tapped into a spiritual realm that has seen the depths of humanity's desperation. You have extended compassion to a grieving mother. You have spoken to a God who will kneel to listen, and regardless of whether or not you received the desired result, this is something of incredible value.

Blessings cannot always be synonymous with transparent, crystal-clear waters. Sometimes they're obscured by our circumstances, rendering them difficult to spot, much like the flower paintings that adorned those hospital hallways in the labor and delivery wing. Just because I had failed to notice them while I agonized through childbirth did not mean the beauty had not always been there, surrounding me.

We will always struggle to see blessings in the midst of tragedy the same way we will wrestle with a God who allows tragedy to strike us. This is normal. I might even argue that this is itself a blessing, for from this place grows humility.

We often believe that we are more merciful than God, that we must safeguard his reputation, that we must convince him to be as good, loving, and patient as we are. Sometimes that leads us to lament, one of the most appropriate responses to suffering. The Bible tells us all of creation groans for God's goodness to be revealed. The blood of the innocent cries out to him. We see this desire encapsulated in Abraham's plea in Genesis 18:25:

"Far be it from you to do such a thing, to put the righteous to death with the wicked, so that the righteous fare as the wicked! Far be that from you! Shall not the Judge of all the earth do what is right?"

Other times we separate ourselves from the worst aspects of humanity — from the genocides, the wars, the brutality. We don't identify with those horrific acts and we have fallen out of the habit of acknowledging collective sin. We build chasms between ourselves and the evil we see, casting blame on a different time or a different culture. But it's us. It's humanity. In our attempt to police God's goodness, we fail to recognize our role in the injustice we want vindicated. You may beg God to judge the world, but you never expect him to start with you. God becomes the surgeon who cannot operate on the tumor without jeopardizing the very life he wants to save.

I never bypassed the problem of pain in the pursuit of spirituality. I simply underestimated its powerful ability to bring attention to the hidden cancers inside us, operating like the radioactive medication that causes tumors to shine in a PET scan. The suffering I endured directly challenged my ability to arrive on the same page as the mind of God. I considered myself an understanding person, one who could shift an object in my hands multiple different ways to consider every perspective. I thought I had the intellectual ability to entertain God's purposes, whether through my own knowledge of his character or through my own capacity for wisdom. In the sickness and suffering and death of my child, I simply could not meet him there. I learned that I was not as accepting as I thought I was. I was not as rational as I thought I was. I was not as impressive or long-suffering as I thought I was. There were indeed limitations on which trials I would allow into my life. There were puzzles I couldn't solve and battles my logic couldn't fight. Where I thought I'd find humility, I found pride. Where I thought I'd find obedience, I found defiance. Where I thought I'd find praise, I found entitlement.

And so it is with all of us.

You are one bad circumstance away from becoming the very thing you think you are above. Whether that be financial hardship, poor health, a weak marriage, a depressive episode, or a cruel character — believe me, the seed is already planted in your heart. It just needs water. It just needs the right conditions.

God continues to lead us into tribulations, painfully extracting that which rots our bones. You'd be surprised what is brought to the surface from a little applied pressure. You can decide on your own whether these painful procedures make him a heartless tyrant or a life-saving physician.

I will never fully comprehend God's plans or his ways, and perhaps that's a good thing. How big could the God of the universe be if I could contain all of him within my finite mind? The Bible is full of chapters in which people pour out their complaints to a God they struggle to comprehend in the face of deplorable acts of violence and tragic deaths. These passages can be seen as raw, emotional diary entries, overflowing with anger and frustration. Emotional outbursts with God should not just be tolerated, they should be encouraged. Why? Because they serve as a humbling reminder of our place within the vast universe. It's the proof of our own limitations. It reminds us of the truth that we are not in control. We are not gods but rather creatures made in the image of God. We are limited beings who must grapple with the challenge of understanding a higher mind with higher purposes.

As I waited to be allowed into the PICU, I shoved my trembling hands into my pockets where I had stuffed every burdensome question I couldn't answer. I questioned whether Jude's life would be one of unending suffering. I questioned whether God would back me into a corner. I questioned if and when he would make me kill my own son. It seemed like God had not found his end in our sorrows just yet, and when your child is sick, that is simply beyond your human capacity for understanding. The blessings were difficult, even impossible, to recognize, but I had to believe the song of hope continued to ring true, even if I could no longer hear it.

I doubt this hope permeated the heart of Jesus' mother while she knelt at the foot of the cross. As her son's blood pooled around her while he endured brutal lashes that tore his flesh from his bone, it would be nothing short of human to feel forsaken. I wonder if she recalled hearing his innocent giggles as a baby while he cried out in agony. I wonder if she remembered kissing the same feet they were nailing to a cross. When she could barely meet the eyes of the bloodstained, sacrificial lamb, I wonder if she, too, questioned in anguish. I can only imagine the frustration and heartache all of Jesus' loved ones might have felt when he lowered every sword, refused to resist arrest, and calmly whispered that it must be so. For reasons beyond their comprehension, it must be so. For a greater good that lay beyond their generation, it must be so. For a redemptive plan more vast than they could have ever imagined, it must be so. This hand must be dealt. When we fear that the blessings have run out and that the gold lies only in the past, he reminds us to look beyond what lies in plain sight.

When the security guard granted me access, I made my way to the PICU and took note of how it was on the opposite side of the hospital from the postpartum wing. I was no longer in that euphoric place where joy abounded. I was in the place where the hallways were dark, congratulations were replaced with condolences, and sorrow attached itself to my skin, weighing me down like sopping wet clothes I could never change out of. I had left the place where children were welcomed into this world and entered the place where children came to die.

When I entered Jude's room I found him lying peacefully in his PICU bed, once again reliant on high-flow oxygen. I curled up onto the uncomfortable hospital chair that I had made a home out of. The respiratory therapist gave me the report of Jude's typical near-death-experience and assured me the PICU was the best place for him. How cursed it was that my arms were not the best place for him. How heartbreaking that our home was not the best place for him. The team asked if I wanted to call the intensivist in, but since Jude was looking okay by the time I arrived, I told them to let him sleep. There was nothing he could do for me now anyway.

I had pulled the chair next to Jude and laid my upper body across his bed, my place of worship. Jude stared at me inquisitively, almost as if to ask why I was coming to see him in the middle of the night. I grabbed Jude's hand and counted his fingers like blessings until we fell asleep.

—

In the early morning, I awoke to Dr. M gazing at me and Jude outside the glass windows that lined each PICU room. When my eyes met his, he gestured for me to come outside and I unraveled my creaky, sore body from the hospital chair, trying not to wake up Jude. Due to the severity of Jude's respiratory failure and the fact that he was convulsing and unable to make eye contact during the event, there was more talk about possible seizure activity. Dr. M explained that they wanted to perform another EEG. This would be his fifth one.

I couldn't fault them for it. Seizures would've been expected after a hypoxic brain injury, and it would provide a reasonable explanation for such an extreme desat. I let them do what they had to do. But, after another 48 hours of monitoring, there were no seizures detected. I had already assumed, given the fact that Jude hadn't shown seizure activity for months and he did not display any signs of a postictal phase (altered state of consciousness that commonly follows seizures) after the event.

With no other options left, we had to continue monitoring Jude in the PICU until we could get our hands on a CPAP mask, our last hope. After weeks of searching, our pulmonologist finally managed to find and order one, and it arrived at the end of November.

Our medical team helped us manage our expectations about CPAP. They warned us that it could be noisy, forceful, and highly uncomfortable. Many adults struggled to tolerate CPAP, so it was uncertain that Jude, an irrational infant who could not be reasoned with or even bribed, would take to it easily.

When the equipment arrived, a meeting was held inside Jude's small hospital room, with all the respiratory therapists and our pulmonologist present. They gathered around as a representative from our medical equipment company provided a brief presentation on the ventilator settings and CPAP mask. Nobody had experience with this particular equipment for a baby. It was a tiny nasal mask that created a seal around Jude's nose, but left his mouth open. A long hose clipped into the mask and connected to a ventilator, making Jude look like he had grown an elephant trunk. The ventilator was smaller and sleeker than I was expecting. It had tubing connected to a humidifier filled with water that always needed to be running. The ventilator provided a breathing rate for Jude, meaning it delivered him breaths, which was assuring in case his lungs grew tired or he had an apneic event.

It was a busy day in our hospital room with the new equipment. It wasn't until late afternoon that we could give the CPAP mask a proper trial, but I noticed Jude's heart rate steadily increasing on the monitor. My concern was growing. Once I saw the heart rate reach the 180s and 190s, I asked a nurse to check his temperature. Sure enough, he had a fever. I requested a viral panel, which returned positive for something unexpected — COVID-19.

While COVID-19 typically didn't pose a significant threat to most babies, we had to exercise caution and closely monitor Jude's response. Given his limited ability to cough, even a mild respiratory infection could threaten Jude's life. Due to the high stakes, our doctor decided to administer remdesivir, a drug that inhibits viral replication of COVID. We had to wait to see how Jude would respond to the infection before trialing CPAP.

The next several days were slow and uneventful as

we monitored Jude. Thankfully, COVID did not seem to affect him too severely. His fevers were manageable, and he remained alert. On December 2, it had been exactly 6 months since Jude's cardiac arrest. Since he was doing well, we initiated the CPAP trial, which Jude tolerated nicely. In fact, the added support from the ventilator was likely helpful as he fought the viral infection.

The night of December 2, Jack and I lovingly tucked Jude into his bed, singing him his familiar lullabies just as we always did. I did my best to establish a routine and create a comforting sense of familiarity for him amidst his chaotic life. We never left Jude's side until long after he fell asleep to make sure he didn't wake up searching for us. We stared at the screen showing Jude's vitals until his heart rate was low enough for long enough that I deemed he was fast asleep. His CPAP mask was on but he didn't seem to mind it too much.

I always introduced myself to the night nurse assigned to Jude and briefed any respiratory therapists responsible for administering overnight treatments. We provided them with a thorough overview of Jude's condition, my preferences for medication administration, and suggestions on what to do if he experienced desats. I reminded them to call me if Jude ever woke up in the night, writing my number all over the whiteboard (even though I knew they already had it documented). The response was often a reassuring hand on our shoulders and a soft whisper, "Just try to get some rest."

We said goodnight to the familiar hospital staff who had become an integral part of our lives at this point and made our way home. It was a dark and rainy night. Jack and I silently trudged into our apartment, following our customary routine of heating up dinner around 10 p.m. before heading to bed. Thankfully, our church had set up a meal train for us and placed a cooler outside our front door where people could drop off a dinner for us to eat by the time we got home from the hospital. These people were truly angels among us. If it weren't for them, I would be sustained by cereal. I tried not to stay up too late, not only because I needed to wake up early to return to the hospital, but also because I still had to wake up several times throughout the night to pump breast milk for Jude.

I dragged myself into bed and listened to the rain softly pattering on the roof. Our bedroom was dark and felt empty. I told myself to just get through one more day, as I always did. I said a prayer for Jude and fell asleep staring at his empty bassinet. Soon after I drifted off, the phone rang.

My stomach dropped.

—

I hydroplaned on the slick, black freeway as I raced almost as fast as my heart to get to the hospital. In the passenger seat, my husband, stressed and sleep-deprived, sat with his head in his hands, demanding to know why this had to happen.

Jude had suffered another cardiac arrest.

It happened precisely six months after his first one, almost to the hour. If this is all starting to feel like a cruel joke to you, believe me, it did to us as well.

When I ran into the PICU, an ominous scene greeted me — Jude's hospital room surrounded with medical staff. It's never a good sign when that happens. We had to throw on gowns and masks before entering because Jude was technically in a quarantine room for his virus. The assistant who fetched the gowns for us was the same one who regularly helped us bathe Jude. She was so fun-loving and always brought a vibrant spirit to Jude's hospital room. She usually spoke to him in Spanish, telling jokes and poking at his chubby rolls while Jude gazed at her with wide eyes. Now, her hands trembled while she handed us our gowns. Her head hung in despair, like she couldn't bare to look at us in the eyes. I took the gown from her and was about to walk away when she softly spoke.

"Taylor I'm so sorry," she choked. I turned to look at her. She was silent for a moment. "I'm just so sorry this is happening to you."

I stared at her and tried to give a weak smile, but I'm not so sure I was strong enough.

Jack and I quikcly put on the gowns and masks so we could get to Jude. The nurse who called me on the phone hadn't provided much information because she was a pediatric nurse down the hall, but we assumed it must have been a severe desat, one that required resuscitation efforts. However, our confusion grew when the team revealed it wasn't a respiratory issue.

In the dimly lit room, we stood beside Jude, who gazed silently at us, breathing normally. I held his hand, unbelievably grateful he was still alive. The nurse explained that shortly after we left, Jude's IV had broken, and the IV team had been brought in with an ultrasound machine to find another vein. I was already upset about this because there was no reason they needed to replace an IV overnight while he was sleeping and when no one was there to comfort him. The IV was primarily for administering his remdesivir and Jude had already gotten his dose for the night, so the new IV could've easily waited until morning.

Jude was fast asleep when the IV team was gliding the ultrasound machine over Jude's legs in search of another vein. Our nurse was monitoring the screen and noticed Jude's heart rate beginning to fall. Before he could even comprehend what was happening, Jude's heart rate plummeted inexplicably, setting off all the alarms. The IV team checked their screen and could see that Jude had lost his pulse completely. Our nurse immediately started CPR and called code blue. Luckily, Jude's heart rate was restored in less than a minute.

Surprisingly, it wasn't Jude's lungs this time. He was satting at 100 before his arrest. They informed us that the intensivist was already on his way, which was good news because we had a handful of questions. Did Jude actually have a heart issue all along? Could that be possible? After six months of exhaustive tests, monitoring, and hospitalization, could we have missed something?

Our doctor arrived and requested a meeting with us in the conference room.

There, the three of us sat in that same cursed conference room. I pressed my trembling hands into the worn wooden table and fixated my gaze on the large digital clock, its red numbers blinking above the doctor's head. The last time I had seen that clock, it had read June 2, 2022, and Jude's comatose body was just down the hall. Now, it read December 2, 2022. Half a year later, yet we sat in the same spot.

Jude had survived the initial injury, but only for the shadow of death to lurk in the corner ever since. In every sense of the word, I was exhausted. I did my best to keep my bloodshot eyes locked on death's shadow that had followed us day and night. I was terrified of what it might do if I let it out of my sight, but it felt like my body was failing me with its demands of sleep. Each time my cement eyelids couldn't hold open any longer, death would screech at the top of its lungs — a sound so horrific, so piercing, like a freight train hurtling toward me as I had fallen asleep at the wheel. Adrenaline courses through my entire body as my eyes snap open, I grip the edge of my seat and gasp for air. Once again, death veers away at the last minute, cackling with amusement.

Death is satisfied, for it has made me flinch once more. It has proven its power over me time and time again. It retreats back into the corner, lying in wait, assuring me with a wicked smile that I needn't worry, I can surely rest my weary eyes now.

8

Thy Will Be Done

"The LORD has made everything for its purpose, even the wicked for the day of trouble."
- Proverbs 16:4 (ESV)

The discussion in the conference room with our doctor included many questions and not a lot of answers. Like many times before, we discussed how we could possibly move forward in light of these ever increasing life-threatening events. We couldn't live in a sea of code blue. We couldn't keep teetering on this tightrope any longer.

When I asked our doctor if we needed to broach the topic of hospice care, he told me it was not an inappropriate time to start that conversation. Prior to this event, someone else on our medical team had also suggested placing Jude in a sub-acute care facility (which I would have never done). Though we hadn't officially talked about it, there was a tone among our team that suggested Jude's unexplained respiratory failures and dramatically declining lung health were starting to become too heavy for them to carry. They had lost hope and I could read it on their faces.

To rule out a cardiac issue, our doctor ordered another EKG and blood tests to check for any electrolyte imbalances. I remained convinced that Jude's heart was fine.

In the morning, the hospital's pediatric cardiologist

reviewed Jude's telemetry (recordings from his vitals) from the night of the cardiac arrest, along with his EKGs and previous echoes, and almost immediately ruled out any heart problems.

I had a strong hunch that the culprit might be remdesivir, a drug known to lower heart rates. Jude's heart rates consistently dropped after receiving the medication, and I requested that it be discontinued following his cardiac arrest. Since COVID didn't appear to be significantly affecting him, I believed that any potential benefits of the drug were not worth the risk. Thankfully, our medical team agreed, although it took some time for everyone to come to a consensus, given the gravity of the situation. One doctor remained skeptical, arguing that Jude would be the first reported case of such a reaction to remdesivir. However, we had spoken to traveling nurses in the PICU who had witnessed remdesivir causing dangerously low heart rates in babies multiple times before.

Another point of contention arose when one doctor suggested that Jude's recent cardiac arrest might have been caused by the CPAP mask he was wearing at the time. This doctor theorized that the positive pressure was pushing secretions into Jude's airway, causing him to choke. Jack vehemently disagreed and I didn't blame him. He refused to let this unfounded theory jeopardize the only option we had left that could allow Jude to go home, especially since CPAP had previously benefited Jude. The doctor insisted that Jude couldn't trial CPAP as long as he had COVID, and we had to reluctantly wait, despite our disagreements. If the issue was an obstructed airway, you would expect to see a patient exhibit some signs of respiratory distress before their heart rate fell to the floor and they lost a pulse, but we couldn't spin our wheels trying to win every argument.

After allowing Jude to fully recover from COVID

without remdesivir, we were safe to begin his CPAP trial again. Jude was tolerating it quite well. However, one major concern remained: we had no clarity on how many hours a day Jude needed to be on the CPAP for it to be effective. Ideally, he could wear it only while sleeping at night and during naps, but there was a chance he might require it all the time. We counted ourselves fortunate if Jude could tolerate brief breaks from it during the day. Although the CPAP was undoubtedly keeping his lungs open, we couldn't predict how quickly they would collapse once we removed the support.

Praise the Lord that, over time, we were able to gradually reduce Jude's reliance on his 24/7 CPAP and ventilator support. We followed a painstakingly slow yet consistent schedule of weaning Jude off hour by hour. Eventually, he only needed it during nap time and overnight. Outside of those hours, Jude could maintain his oxygen levels with just 1.5 liters of oxygen delivered through a low-flow nasal cannula. He hadn't been on that little oxygen support since we had left CHLA. Given Jude's history of unpredictable desats, we knew that the medical team would require a substantial amount of data before feeling confident that this approach was successful. We knew that Jude would need to be monitored at this level of support for at least another month. Sadly, it meant that we would likely be stepping into the new year still in the hospital. It was disheartening, but it brought us one step closer to taking him home.

And so, Jude grew. The seasons changed outside hospital windows. We set up a small Christmas tree next to Jude and opened presents on Christmas morning. It was during last year's Christmas that we had publicly announced our pregnancy with Jude. Jack and I were in awe that, by next Christmas, we would have a little baby with us.

I had envisioned what our first Christmas with our

baby would look like. It wasn't this. Thankfully, we can trust God even with our disappointments. When we have our own ideas of how life should play out, it's a difficult task to accept God's will, not to merely receive it. Receiving is the action we do when we have been given something, but accepting is the response of taking it. To accept implies a recognition of value and a degree of willingness, while receiving simply refers to the act of obtaining. In this way, we receive God's will when we hold it with a reluctant act of obedience because we know we have no other choice.

None of us would willingly choose a path of thorns, and yet, sometimes, that is the path God has given us. To accept God's will is to know it has been permitted by the creator of the stars and the seas. To accept God's will is to trust him with the grand narrative of humanity, knowing there is no violence or death or illness powerful enough to change the ending. Until the time has come that God himself has ordained, you have purpose here. Trusting God empowers you to welcome God's will with open arms, rather than merely receiving it out of necessity. My baby's first Christmas wasn't what I had expected, but it was what God had given. The follower of Christ can boldly place his feet on the path of death, knowing even this will ultimately lead to the path of life.

—

The hospital's infectious disease specialist came to visit us one day after thoroughly reviewing Jude's medical history. She had some questions, particularly regarding the urinary tract infection (UTI) that Jude had on the night of his initial cardiac arrest in June. We had consulted various infectious disease doctors at CHLA because the UTI was one of the few abnormalities we could pinpoint at the time his heart stopped. What made it unusual was that Jude's UTI was caused by staphylococcus aureus, which isn't typically associated with UTIs. She began to explain this to us, and we mentioned that we had discussed it with other doctors in the past. They had conducted blood tests and even performed a lumbar puncture on Jude to examine his spinal fluid, and we didn't see any sign of infection anywhere outside his urine. Still, she pointed out that the quantity of blood taken from Jude was too small for a reliable sample. Jude was only 11 days old that night, so they were limited on how much blood they could take. We had taken additional blood tests at CHLA, but they had been conducted about 24 hours after Jude was put on broad-spectrum antibiotics, so it wasn't surprising that they didn't find anything. The presence of staphylococcus aureus isolated in Jude's urine was more than just unusual — it was unheard of.

"It's a bacteria that lives on our skin. For it to get in his urine, it would have had to crawl up the urinary tract and it simply just doesn't do that," she explained. "You only find UTIs caused by this bacterium in less than one percent of cases, and in those cases it's almost always introduced by a foley catheter."

Jude never had a catheter before his hospitalization. The chances of Jude having this infection isolated in his urine were so low, she almost considered it biologically impossible.

"This bacterium starts in the bloodstream," she went on. "I think Jude was septic the night of June 2, and it led to his cardiac arrest."

"But we have no evidence of that," I said.

"The evidence is that your perfectly healthy baby's heart stopped," she said firmly. "Neonates can turn septic in a matter of minutes."

Although we could never turn back time to prove it, it was the closest thing we had to closure. As I thought back on Jude's hospitalization, I began connecting the dots of this mysterious UTI that had always been a perplexing piece of the puzzle. The first week at CHLA, no one knew how to interpret it. Our initial attending doctor had mentioned that she would consider it a significant factor if we couldn't find an alternative explanation. Our pediatrician, who kept in touch with us throughout Jude's entire hospitalization, always believed that dismissing it as a mere coincidence was absurd.

It was not only the fact that it was caused by such an unlikely and strange bacterium, but it was also oddly resistant to treatment. Despite the strong antibiotics he was receiving at CHLA, we repeatedly detected this bacterium in his urine throughout the first week. It had reached a point where they conducted ultrasounds of his kidneys because other infectious disease specialists suspected he might have an abscess that the medication wasn't reaching.

Revisiting the night of June 2 caused me to reflect on that night. I thought about the moments that led up to this life-changing event. Jack and I were driving to our friends' house, Jude was crying in his car seat as I sat beside him. Normally, he would settle down once we started driving, but not this time. I'll always remember Jack glancing at me in the rear view mirror as he came to a stop at a red light. His brown eyes studied me as I tried to soothe Jude. He suggested we turn back home. Jack put on his blinker and positioned his hands on the wheel to prepare for a turn, but I told him to keep going. I thought Jude would calm down soon enough.

I often wondered if things would have turned out differently if I had just said okay. If I had just let Jack take a u-turn like he wanted to. If we had just headed home. Would we have avoided all of this? Would we have escaped a tragic, split-second moment that led to our child's life being permanently altered? It's possible. But if the infection that later led to Jude's heart stopping had already been progressing toward sepsis, it's impossible to say for certain what could have occurred. What if we had gone home? What if we tucked him into bed for a nap? Living in an apartment 15 minutes away from the nearest hospital and considering what modern medicine can provide for an asystolic patient, it doesn't bode well. In visiting our friends' house, we placed ourselves literally down the street from an emergency room, the closest we ever got in our daily lives.

Regardless of the initial cause of Jude's heart stopping, it was an extraordinarily unlikely and unfortunate event. As we neared the end of our long journey in the ICU, I felt a weight lifted as I pondered God's will. What if this life-or-death decision I made at a red light all those months ago wasn't an awful shame, after all? What if it was our saving grace?

—

In January, our PICU team finally felt confident enough to transfer Jude back to the pediatric wing. The pediatric team was understandably hesitant, given that every previous encounter they had with Jude required intensive care. It took some convincing by our PICU team for them to take Jude because they technically did not accept patients still on a CPAP/BiPAP machine. They had to make an exception for Jude, as this was the support he would need when going home. It was the first case the team had of something like this. There was a long history of making exceptions for Jude.

When we arrived at the pediatric wing, we were feeding Jude continuously, as he still had occasional difficulties tolerating his milk. I had long given up on that particular battle. My sole concern was ensuring he received proper nourishment without compromising his respiratory status, something that was seemingly stable for the first time. We were so close to the end now, I barely spoke of it. Making it to a discharge day was like catching butterflies. I had to be steady, slow, silent. I feared it would disappear in an instant if I made a sudden movement. After all, positive news had often proved illusory in the past.

During the holidays, Jack's family and some friends moved all of our belongings from our old apartment to a new, one-story apartment in the same complex. This new apartment was still on the university's campus, but it had a more open floor plan, no stairs, and plenty of storage space for Jude's machines and supplies. We began making calls to a nursing agency and started scheduling at-home nursing care to assist with Jude's needs. We even met with a couple agency managers in Jude's hospital room to provide detailed information about his case and medical requirements. Like everyone else, they were surprised to see Jude so alert. I felt a growing sense of excitement, not just because we might finally get to go home but because this time, we weren't going it alone.

In other historical news, Jack and I became the first parents to receive training on how to use an Ambu bag. Despite the promising outlook with the CPAP mask maintaining open lungs for Jude, his condition remained highly unpredictable. His lungs could collapse at any moment, but our hope was that, with time, Jude would grow stronger. The Ambu bag delivers positive pressure ventilation through a bag valve mask connected to an oxygen tank. Typically, this equipment was reserved for trained medical personnel like paramedics or doctors during emergency situations. It served as a constant reminder that, no matter how well Jude was doing, no one considered his life safe, and we always had to be prepared for the worst-case scenario.

On January 10, 2023, it was discharge day. Jude had

been on CPAP for nearly a month with no desat events, the longest he had ever gone in his hospitalization. Once Jack and I secured home nursing, our team was ready to send us on our way. We had met with every specialist and packed up all of Jude's things. Jack had gone out to the car to drop off the last of the boxes when one of our favorite respiratory therapists dropped by, the same one who worked on Jude in his most recent ER visit several months ago. She wasn't assigned to the pediatric floor that day, so she went out of her way to see us before we left. She was a compassionate person with a loud laugh and a soft soul, but my favorite part about her was that she referred to my son as Jude, not as the room number he was assigned to. I'm sure they do that for patient privacy, but it secured her a special place in my heart nonetheless.

"How do you feel?" she asked me, brushing Jude's curls off his forehead. We assumed our typical positions, she on one side of Jude's hospital bed and me on the other.

I told her how our physical therapist and occupational therapist had already visited and given us the recommendations for Jude's services moving forward.

"I'm sure you will give him the best," she said with a smile.

It was silent for a moment as I chewed on my lip. The setting sun cast the room in a dreary orange haze. One huge benefit of this hospital was that every room had a window, so I avoided ever turning on artificial light in order to help Jude's circadian rhythm.

"I'll try my hardest," I said. "I just want to make sure I balance it all well."

"What do you mean?" she asked.

"I just don't ever want to unintentionally communicate to him that he's not okay the way that he is," I said.

She tilted her head at me, listening intently.

"I mean...I'm going to do everything I can to help him walk, talk, eat. But if he can't do those things..." I trailed off. "...if he can't do those things, that's okay. I want him to know it's okay if he can't. I don't want to be a parent that pushes him just because I'm unwilling to see his own limitations. I want him to know I see him as he is, and it's okay."

I was preparing myself to lift my palms upward and accept, not just receive, whatever hard and holy things God had in store for me. I knew it would be painful. I knew how likely it was that Jude would struggle with disabilities his entire life. I knew there might not be any more milestones to witness. I knew I might never see him grow up. I knew this life would require me to leave bloody and beaten dreams to die along the side of the road.

Still, I believed God would give me the strength to grasp at it with both hands, holding all its ugliness and brokenness, all its grief and all its hardships, and say,

"So be it. I accept you."

She was quiet a few moments longer before whispering the word "wow" under her breath as she shook her head and walked around Jude's bed to give me a hug.

"You're a really great mom," she whispered to me.

—

After 220 days in the hospital, our 7 ½-month-old baby was finally ready to go home for good. The hospital hallways were lined with nurses, doctors, and respiratory therapists as we wheeled Jude out in the stroller he had barely had a chance to use. They cheered and threw confetti, waving goodbye to us with tears in their eyes and beaming faces. It was a surreal moment, different from the last time. This time, I felt ready. Jude was ready. His chest x-rays showed clear lungs and he was on low oxygen support. I was exhausted from watching

him grow up in the hospital.
It was time for us to go home.

9

Healing Waits For You

"Believe in the light while you have the light, so that you may become children of light."
- John 12:36 (NIV)

Arriving home brought about a complex mix of emotions. It was a relief to be in a new, clean space, free from the memories of a life we could never return to. I could never accurately express how significant it was that our friends prepared our home for us beforehand. The fact that they organized our pantry, assembled our furniture, and hung new plants that they had purchased for us is the embodiment of letting the light in for someone who can't do it themselves.

Still, it was heart-wrenching in many ways. I couldn't shake the ache I felt when I set Jude down to bed, surrounded by machines, listening to the sound of the ventilator breathing for him. I've come to realize that was just grief in another form. There was still a part of me that felt hopeless and worried incessantly about the possibility that Jude would never be fully independent from a ventilator and what that would mean for him.

Despite the lingering sadness, this part right here — this was the best part. The part between hospital walls and a funeral home. The part where Jude got a taste of all the life he had not yet known.

We met our nursing staff on the evening we arrived home from the hospital and began training them on Jude's daily care. Simultaneously, we were developing a routine for Jude and an intricate system to manage all his medical needs. Jude required constant supervision, especially during car rides when I was driving him to his appointments, so having a nurse was incredibly helpful as Jack returned to his graduate program.

We wasted no time in setting up Jude's support systems. We had copious notes about the various programs, services, and therapies available to us, and we had to carefully balance them with Jude's other specialist appointments. The hospital's therapists recommended "high- frequency" therapy for Jude, as they had become increasingly optimistic about his progress over the last few months. Jude started receiving occupational and physical therapy twice a week. After an infant motor scale test, the therapists placed Jude in the most severe category. They assured us not to worry too much, as it would be challenging to discern what was due to brain damage and what was delayed because he spent his entire life in a hospital room. The therapists' optimism was a breath of fresh air, especially after being immersed in a deficit-oriented medical environment.

To the untrained eye, Jude was beginning to resemble a normal baby more and more. He was sitting unassisted, smiling, and even had his own unique laugh that we found so endearing. It was like a mix between a grunt and a gurgle, sometimes punctuated with little hiccup noises in between. Jude was social and fully aware of his surroundings. He was using both his hands and steadily expanding his range of motion every week.

If anyone was ever dedicated to anything, it was I to Jude's development. It was a devotion that was finally set free like a lion from a cage. For so long, there were so many limitations holding me back. I couldn't play with Jude the way I wanted to. I couldn't show him nature the way I wanted to. I couldn't challenge him the way I wanted to. I couldn't even hold him when I wanted to. For seven months, I had to watch obstacles pile up in his path, waiting and praying for the day when I could help him move them.

Now that I didn't have to ask for permission, I began weaning Jude off daytime oxygen almost immediately. With the CPAP and BiPAP machine maintaining his lung function, he no longer needed the extra oxygen support during the day. I wanted to start weaning Jude off his oxygen during his last few weeks in the hospital, but all the doctors refused to make any changes for fear of jeopardizing his progress. I preferred that Jude not have oxygen because it masked signs of respiratory distress. If Jude's lungs were starting to collapse, I wouldn't know right away if we were supplementing him with oxygen. However, when he wasn't on oxygen, his SpO_2 would drop if his lungs were collapsing, signaling that he needed more time on his ventilator, which was ultimately the only thing that helped him. Although I understood Jude's dependency on modern medicine, I was also eager to disconnect him from any machines or tubing whenever possible. When I took off Jude's nasal cannula, it was the first time since he was a newborn that I could see my son's face free from masks, tape and tubing. His cheeks were blistered and red from having tape on them for almost his entire life.

In addition to Jude's physical therapy and occupational therapy, he also received craniosacral therapy, feeding therapy and speech therapy. The feeding and speech therapy were quite similar at his age, primarily focused on providing him with oral stimulation. Jude had spent almost his entire life being fed through a tube, so he had no concept of eating. Muscles tend to atrophy when not in use, so it was crucial to regularly encourage oral muscle movement. Sadly, Jude had developed a severe oral aversion due to all the trauma he had endured, making it an uphill battle to overcome his fear and resistance to allowing anything in his mouth.

With appointments scheduled almost every day of the week, Jude became my full-time job. It was important to me to create a routine for him as a sense of comfort. I took him on walks nearly every day, introducing him to flowers, trees, and ocean waves. His poor blue eyes were always squinting in response to sunlight he had barely ever seen before.

One of my favorite parts of the day was bath time, strategically scheduled after feeding therapy and before bedtime. Even before Jude would allow anything into his mouth, I exposed him to food and encouraged him to interact with it, which often resulted in a mess. During most of Jude's time in the hospital, we could only give him wipe-downs, and we eventually progressed to sponge baths in the last couple of months. Still, it required a few people because of all the equipment.

At home, I would get into the bathtub with Jude almost every night. It was mainly because we didn't have a baby bathtub, and I needed to hold him, but it was also a precious gift to lay him across my chest while pouring warm water over his back. Jude would typically be soothed right to sleep, and during those moments, I remembered the days in the hospital when I would thank God for even a few minutes when Jude was not in pain or crying. These serene moments became my favorite way to end each day.

As the weeks passed and he got older, bath time became a bit more active, and it was a rare occurrence for him to fall asleep against my chest. He became too busy reaching for every bottle and toy in his line of sight. I've never been so happy to clean up spilled shampoo. It was as if everyday was a miracle — every mess was a masterpiece in my eyes. I couldn't believe he could reach, grasp, sit, and smile. The funny thing is, these milestones for Jude were still quite delayed, as his skill set measured in at around that of a five-month-old when he was nearly nine months old. But I had no frame of reference for these "small things" to be routine or mundane. The fact that I could even lie with him, even for just a few moments, without any machines attached to him was enough for me.

As Jude became less dependent on equipment, he began to roll. His first roll triggered lots of shrieking and squealing on my end, as I didn't know if he would ever be capable of such a thing. We were so used to months of specialists and therapists assessing Jude and noting how he wasn't reaching, wasn't tracking, and wasn't responding to his environment. Soon, rolling became his main means of exploration. Unlike most parents, we didn't have to worry about him ever getting into things or putting stuff in his mouth, but as he grew, he started reaching for things around him. Each bit of normalcy that leaked into our lives felt like an overflow of blessings.

In February, we had Jude's first appointment with an ENT (ears, nose, and throat) doctor. It was the first time this doctor had met Jude, and she observed him in silence for a few minutes while I entertained him with books. Jude adored books more than anything, so I always took a few with me to prepare for the long hours in waiting rooms.

"Has he had a swallow study done?" she asked me.

I looked up at her, surprised. Everyone had told me not to even think about a swallow study for Jude until he was at least a toddler. Most thought it was a terrible idea to do a swallow study on an infant who couldn't even manage to swallow his own spit.

"No," I said. "I would love one, but no one has agreed to do one for me."

After observing Jude, she couldn't believe that he had no swallow. She mentioned that she had worked with kids who had no swallow, and they looked nothing like Jude. On one hand, I was delighted that she wanted to arrange a swallow study for him, but on the other hand, it's challenging to determine what brain damage looks like at his age and Jude's looks were deceiving. One of our PICU doctors once said it was almost as if Jude's brain damage skipped his cortex entirely and mainly affected his brain stem. This was because Jude had life-threatening issues with reflexes and apnea, while so many other aspects of him seemed perfectly normal.

Either way, I embraced the opportunity for the swallow study. I became incredibly proactive with Jude's oral stimulation exercises and feeding therapies. Our feeding therapist technically had to sign off on the swallow study, and I could tell she was hesitant to do so because she hadn't seen evidence yet of Jude exhibiting any kind of swallow reflex. She said she sometimes thought she could hear a swallow, but she couldn't feel one. Still, I wanted to gather information about what was happening anatomically when we put something in his mouth. Even though I wasn't expecting Jude to swallow effectively, I believed it would still offer helpful information about what he was specifically struggling with.

For a whole month leading up to the study in late March, I fasted and prayed. I was extremely nervous on the day of the study and tried to keep my expectations in check. To conduct the swallow study, a speech-language pathologist would administer barium in various consistencies for Jude to swallow, while an x-ray technician filmed the process in real time. Several outcomes could be observed, such as a delayed swallow, residue left in the throat indicating a weak swallow, or, worst of all, complete aspiration, where food or liquid enters the windpipe and lungs without any attempt to protect the airway. Of course with you or I, we would gag or cough involuntarily if food or water were going down into our windpipe, but I worried Jude didn't have these reflexes.

We began by offering Jude a small amount of breast milk from a syringe, which I administered. Since Jude couldn't suck and had poor oral coordination skills, I couldn't simply give him a bottle. Surprisingly, the speech-language pathologist reported that Jude had managed to swallow a small amount of breast milk. I had been convinced that liquid, being the most challenging substance to swallow, would be the part he would fail. Next, we gave him barium mixed with mashed peas and avocado I had prepared earlier that day. This mixture had a thick, pasty consistency and should have been the easiest for Jude to swallow.

Initially, I attempted to feed him with a spoon, but the x-ray showed that while Jude's tongue was making the right movements, he struggled to move the mixture to the back of his throat and ended up spitting out most of it. Since Jude couldn't swallow for so long, his brain adapted by learning to simply push everything out of his mouth rather than to swallow it down.

Just when it seemed that Jude might not swallow anything at all, I tried a feeder I had brought from home. It resembled a large silicone pacifier with holes, allowing me to place the entire thing in Jude's mouth, and the food would slowly leak out on the back of his tongue. It was something I often used at home with cut-up fruit or avocado so that Jude could experience the taste of food without the risk of choking on it.

When we tried this method, Jude continued to push most of the food out of his mouth but did manage to demonstrate a small, safe swallow of the food that reached far enough back. Both Jack and I were ecstatic. Our expectations had been exceeded — Jude could swallow. Although the study showed his oral coordination was poor and he spit out most of what went into his mouth, it proved that he technically had the ability. This was crucial because coordination was something therapy could theoretically help, but there wasn't much hope for a complete lack of swallow because no one can activate the part of the brain stem responsible for triggering one. For the first time, Jude was no longer marked NPO (nothing by mouth), and I was cleared to begin trying to feed some of his calories by mouth.

With all the positive progress Jude was making, the balloon of hope continued to swell in everyone's eyes. It was such a slow yet jarring transition from a time when everyone was telling us how terrible Jude looked to a point when all of our therapists were trying to convince us how remarkable Jude's progress was. They almost began scoffing at the thought of cerebral palsy and believed Jude would be crawling in no time. We went from being told that Jude might never eat by mouth to having a feeding therapist comfortably predict that Jude would eventually get off the feeding tube. In fact, he was doing better than most any patient she had worked with before.

Since coming home, Jude was truly thriving. His primary challenge was tolerating his g-tube feeds, which is why I was so determined to start feeding him orally. When he wasn't relying on the tube in his stomach, he seemed to hold down his food better. Jack and I often wondered if it was the body's way of rejecting such a foreign method of eating. After all, the mouth is the first part of the digestive tract, and g-tube feeds bypassed all of that.

Jude even began attempting to pick up food and bring it to his mouth, a huge milestone for a baby who had barely ever eaten before. The therapists were telling us he was a completely different baby than the one he was in the hospital.

We reduced our at-home nursing hours to just around 10 hours a week because Jude was improving so much. At first, we qualified for over 100 hours a week given Jude's medical complexity. He required less suctioning and his respiratory status was stable enough that I even felt comfortable driving short distances alone with him, something I never thought would be possible.

We transitioned to bolus feeding Jude his milk, which meant he wasn't connected to a feeding pump all the time as he used to be. He was now free from oxygen tubes, feeding pumps, and even his pulse oximeter. His oxygen levels consistently remained above 98, and we no longer felt the need to have him constantly hooked up to monitors. Additionally, we only used his CPAP and BiPAP machines overnight while he slept.

There were so many times I grew tired of hearing that Jude didn't turn out like people expected. I was tired of hearing he didn't respond like they had hoped. I remember at CHLA when therapists would come to visit Jude and realize he was almost impossible to work with. One therapist in particular would always leave the room, shaking her head, whispering the same expression: "Shame, shame."

Although Jude's life went against the odds in tragic ways, he beat the odds in miraculous ways as well. Less than 2% of people survive an asystolic cardiac arrest. Jude's brain was starved of oxygen for at least half an hour, and yet, we couldn't find one hint of structural damage in his brain. Where we should have been studying his brain scans to show evidence of cell death, we were marveling at the absence of strokes. After Jude's cardiac arrest, his Glasgow Coma Scale was 3, the lowest possible score. Both his pupils were fixed and non-responsive to light. Every doctor will tell you this presentation shows no appreciable chance of survival.

But Jude survived.

Not only this, he lived. He lived a life I never thought possible. His development exceeded all our expectations and I did everything in my power to support his potential. He gradually weaned off nearly all the support he once so desperately needed. Between his doctor's visits and therapy appointments, red flags began disappearing. Our Ambu bag collected dust in our closet. We established a routine, a feat I had been highly doubtful of ever achieving with such a medically complex child. But we had done it. We had created a sustainable life for ourselves and for Jude.

To embrace these blessings, I had to release the temptation to cling to what had been lost. In a way, I had to mourn the death of the life Jude once had. I had to mourn who he could have been, and who he was before this terrible thing happened to him. Whatever pain you have endured, you must allow healing into. Pain violently rips through our life, but healing is much more polite. Healing will knock, but it will not enter without being invited in. The trials that come will not ask for permission. However, you must resist the temptation to extend the suffering beyond what is necessary. Those who have experienced loss often hold onto pain like a souvenir, they wear it like a badge of honor. In the vast void of grief, it becomes the last thing they can cling to. They fear that healing is synonymous with forgetting, so they persistently pick at the scab until it bleeds anew. Sometimes their weapon of choice is comparison, sometimes guilt, sometimes they trap themselves in an endless loop of "what if?" Reopening the wound is a hopeless attempt to halt time, to align their shattered world with the one that continues to spin.

Much like our experience when we brought Jude home from the hospital, things may eventually become more manageable for you. It's okay to let that happen. It's okay to smile. You don't need to hold the pain so close — it's not going anywhere. Grief is our most faithful companion. Even on days when you find yourself operating without its overbearing presence, you will accidentally touch it, like a hot stove. It will always be there, reminding you.

In the beginning of this book, I likened losing Jude to the Great Red Spot, consuming the entire planet. It's tempting to subscribe to the belief that we live in a grief-illiterate world, that our storms are bigger than what anyone on this planet can comprehend. A common way we make our hot stove feel even hotter is by telling ourselves we are the only ones to experience the pain of fire. We aren't. I am not the first person to experience loss, and I certainly won't be the last. In fact, there will always be someone else's cataclysmic storm that dwarfs ours.

In 1658, an English writer John Evelyn and his wife Mary lost their son. Their son's name was Richard. John and Mary grieved deeply for their firstborn child. After Richard's death, John wrote in his diary: *"Here ends the joy of my life..."*

After enduring unimaginable pain, John and Mary decided to try for another child. Mary became pregnant with another son, a beacon of hope after the tragedy that had struck their family. Shortly after their second son was born, he died. Together, they had six more children.

Only one of them survived.

We see this heartbreak shared in the life of Elizabeth Duncombe and her husband William Brownlow, an English politician. Between 1638 and 1646, Elizabeth and William had seven children. They saw all of them die. In 1642, William's diary entry read: *"Thou O God hast broken me asunder and shaken me to pieces."*

Our pain often convinces us that we are unique, that nobody else knows suffering like ours. Grief feels like an unbearable burden no one else can fathom, but you are part of a long legacy of individuals who have endured immense hardships on this planet. Even today, there are brothers and sisters weathering their own version of your storm.

Throughout Jude's life, I often felt like God was handing me over to what I feared most. Every turn in the road was a cruel twist of fate. If I reasoned with God that I could accept every losing hand except for one in particular, those were surely the cards he dealt to me.

Those diary entries of bereaved parents prove to us that pain is not only universal, it is immune to expectation or commonality. In 21st Century America, it is statistically unlikely that your child will die. In the 1600s, most parents were bereaved parents. It was not uncommon for people to have several children in hopes that even half would survive into adulthood. The edges of their suffering were not softened by their expectations.

Human experiences are not rare, they are shared. It's easy to think that this grief would feel less heavy if only I were not the only one in my community who lost their child. It's easy to think that this grief would feel less heavy if only Jude hadn't had his cardiac arrest when I was the one holding him. It's easy to think this grief would feel less heavy if only there were more clarity to his story, if only we had more answers. It's easy to think this grief would feel less heavy if only the death was earlier, or later. If only I had called the doctor sooner, if only I could have performed CPR better, if only I could have said something, if only I could have kept my mouth shut, if only, if only...

Suffering stands alone. It does not need your assistance in affliction. We do this so often by adding unnecessary weight to our pain through guilt, pity, anger, or isolation. We tell ourselves things couldn't possibly get worse. We focus on what has been stolen and dismiss what's still in our very hands. I am not suggesting you must always remain reasonable in your pain, for if you're able to do so, you mustn't be in much pain. I am merely pointing out how easy it becomes to create prisons out of our suffering and grief. Refrain from journeying on a downward spiral of false hypotheticals to explain why the pain is so excruciating. The pain is excruciating because grief is heavy. There is nothing else to it. It is heavy if it is your first child and it is heavy if it is your seventh child. It is heavy even if someone understands because there will always be so much they don't understand. It is heavy regardless of where you fall on the bell curve.

It is heavy regardless.

It is heavy.

10

Tree of Life

*"So also you have sorrow now, but I will see you
again, and your hearts will rejoice, and no one will
take your joy from you."*
- John 16:22 (ESV)

On May 22, 2023, Jude turned one year old. We had thrown
a rainbow-themed birthday party for him in our apartment
with invitations that read "Jude is *one* in a million." I created
cards that listed off each of Jude's unique accomplishments
month by month. Jude had the chance to unwrap presents
and watch iridescent bubbles floating in the air. He sat in his
high chair, inspecting his funfetti cupcake and squishing the
icing and rainbow sprinkles between his pudgy fingers. He
stared at the crowd of faces and floating phones surrounding
him, singing him happy birthday. The same people who had
fervently prayed for him now could share in the joy of his
life. The fact that we had reached this one-year milestone
was profoundly emotional for us.

I couldn't help but reflect on the night of September
29 when we first brought Jude home from CHLA. It was the
night I had broken down in tears. At that time, I had never
imagined that we would reach this point. I had assumed that
Jude would slowly deteriorate over time, restricted by the
machines required to keep him alive. Almost a year later, it
felt like we had made it. It felt like we were out of the woods,

like death was no longer looming in the corner. Jude's life, once buried under low expectations of death and decay, was finally exuding hope.

However, there was a little shroud of darkness surrounding the weeks leading up to Jude's birthday. Jude was sick with presumably some kind of virus, leading me to consider canceling his party multiple times. As the days went by, his oxygen requirements began increasing, and we had to set his BiPAP to higher levels during the night. We even began using the BiPAP for his naps, sometimes even when he was awake, and I began to again monitor his vital signs throughout the day.

We visited the pediatrician three times in one month due to Jude's backsliding. I requested broad-spectrum antibiotics just in case an infection was at play, but they had no effect. I stopped his feeding therapy for weeks to ensure it wasn't contributing to his respiratory distress. I even insisted on a chest x-ray to check for any signs of collapsed lungs, but the images didn't show any collapse. However, there were indications of bronchial swelling, typically associated with a viral infection.

Although our pediatrician wasn't overly concerned about Jude's condition, I hated that he still wasn't back to baseline. Jude had experienced a high fever a couple times, higher than what we'd seen before in the hospital. We could manage them with Tylenol, but he was also much more congested than I'd seen him, constantly spitting out a thick, yellow mucus. His heart rate had gone up higher than ever before one night, rising into the 200s when he was fast asleep. We were up late at night on the phone with doctors, trying to decide whether or not we should take Jude to the ER. We made one last visit to the pediatrician on the evening before his birthday party.

"I understand your concern, but honestly, he looks

great," the pediatrician assured us.

She was right. Jude was alert and playful, showing no signs of pneumonia, and his x-rays were fairly clear. He was tolerating his milk exceptionally well, gaining weight, and making remarkable progress in his therapies. He was even beginning to communicate in small ways, like lifting his arms to be picked up and trying to wave hello.

"I just really truly believe that, this time next week, he'll be totally back to normal," she said.

I could see the wave coming on the horizon, and I felt the fear rising within me. It looked like we would be able to pass over it if only we kept charging ahead.

The morning of May 23, Jude woke me up around 5:30 a.m. While his oxygen levels weren't dangerously low, they hadn't yet returned to his baseline, considering the increased oxygen support he was receiving. I removed him from his ventilator, and he appeared to be his usual, cheerful self. After changing him in the other room, I settled into our nursing chair, gently patting his back. He was sounding so congested and I heard him struggle to breathe through the thick mucus. I recalled our pediatrician's suggestion to use the cough assist machine on Jude in the mornings to help clear it out.

I brought Jude into our bedroom and woke up Jack to help me use the cough assist machine because it usually required two people. Cough assist machines are most effective for individuals with trachs because trachs provide a closed system. The machine applies positive and negative pressure, trying to elicit a slight cough. Even though Jude didn't have a trach and didn't cough along with it, every pulmonologist recommended we use it. The pressure variations could still help loosen anything in Jude's lungs, making it easier for him to clear later. We had used the machine several times in the past, but Jude wasn't a fan of it, so we tried to use it sparingly.

Administering the cough assist required placing a mask over Jude's mouth and nose to create a seal, followed by activating the machine, which was synchronized with his breaths. As Jack held Jude in place, I positioned the mask. I waited for Jude's breath to trigger the machine, but it never did. I removed the mask, puzzled by the lack of response. I stared at the screen to see if something was wrong with the settings. It also struck me as odd that Jude wasn't fussing. When I looked to Jude, he was just staring back at me, and I instantly began to worry if he was breathing okay. I sternly told Jack to grab the suction machine.

When Jack left the room, I picked up Jude to take him off his back in case he was struggling with his congestion. When I did, he immediately fell unconscious and went limp in my arms.

Panic.

My screams could have peeled the paint off the walls as I begged for Jack. Jack ran inside the room and Jude was already turning blue. Our fear was reverberating through the air as we frantically placed Jude on the floor. We struggled to secure his pulse oximeter around his toe to monitor his vitals while simultaneously opening his mouth to check for any obstructions. There was nothing there. The pulse oximeter alarmed, casting a flashing red glow over the room as its readings plummeted. The last number I saw was in the 70s, but then it cut out. At first we were desperately trying to reattach the sensor, thinking it wasn't placed correctly. We soon realized it was working fine, it just couldn't pick up a pulse anymore.

The alarm incessantly screamed its warning of impending doom as Jack began yelling Jude's name while administering CPR. He was delivering breaths through the dreaded Ambu bag that he had to dig out of the closet.

My trembling hands struggled to dial 911 through a veil of tears. The phone call with the dispatcher wasn't long, but I remember asking multiple times how much longer we had to wait for the paramedics.

As the dispatcher continued talking Jack through CPR, I caught a glimpse of red lights through the bedroom window. I dropped the phone and ran outside, almost falling to my knees in desperation, my screams slicing the early morning air. The paramedics stormed into the room.

"It's a ped!" the first paramedic yelled to the team as they knelt around Jude, taking over CPR. Ped is short for pediatric.

He wanted his team to know it was a kid.

He was just a kid.

Jack hovered over them, urging them to administer emergency medications because Jude had no heartbeat. They eventually guided us out of the room as a university police officer arrived at our apartment and began asking us questions. I could tell this wasn't her typical frat party noise complaint call. She was tripping over her words and losing her train of thought as she tried to gather information from me, apologizing in between each request.

I made my way to the closet and grabbed Jude's blue medical binder I put together soon after we arrived home from the hospital months ago. I handed it to her, knowing it would provide the information she needed. They worked on Jude for several minutes while we helplessly stood in the living room and the police officer scribbled on her notepad. Jack held me close as he prayed, promising Jude would be okay.

I knew he wasn't.

I thought I would never feel the way I felt when I saw Jude's lifeless body in the backseat of our car on June 2. On some of my worst days, I would recall that night and tell myself that at least I would almost certainly never experience a feeling like that ever again. Standing in my living room as first responders pounded on Jude's chest, I was in shock that I really had to live through this twice. I couldn't believe this poor child had to experience death *twice*, and he was barely a year old.

They transported Jude into the ambulance, issuing orders to each other while continuing CPR. We were escorted into the police officer's car and she drove us to the emergency room. When we arrived at the all too familiar hospital, we rushed into Jude's panic-stricken room. The doctor was shouting commands, a nurse performed CPR with tears streaming down her face, and other medical staff frantically rushed about. The scene was tragically recognizable. Jude had already been intubated and had an IO drilled into his leg to deliver epinephrine and sodium bicarbonate. Sodium bicarbonate can be used in a desperate attempt to offset the overproduction of acid in your bloodstream.

They had us sit outside the room and as soon as I sat down I saw a nurse sprinting over to us from down the hall. It was a nurse from the PICU, one we had grown close to. I immediately flung myself into her arms, thankful to find a sense of familiarity that wasn't agonizing. She cried with me and held my hands as they continued working on Jude. Her face was heavy with sorrow, tears pouring down her cheeks. We exchanged words between sobs as I cried that it was all my fault. She firmly assured me it was not.

They finally allowed us back into the room, where they continued CPR and administered numerous rounds of emergency medications. I know this part. It's the part where they want the parents to come in so they can see how hard the medical team worked to bring back their lifeless child. Jack, still holding onto hope, continued asking if they had found a pulse, if there was any pulse, if he was alive yet. The nurse's response remained consistent: "We would stop CPR if we had a pulse. We will stop the second we can stop."

People flowed in and out of the room, and many faces were familiar to us. Another PICU nurse rushed into the room, one who had frequently cared for Jude and had heard about his admission to the ER. She broke down in tears immediately upon seeing us, and we became a collective, sobbing mess in the corner of the hospital room.

While Jack was still holding on, I knew. This time, there was no naive optimism. Jude couldn't be one a million twice. I knew that even if they could restore a pulse, my son, as I knew him, was gone. Regardless of whether they could revive him, he had gone too long without oxygen. His brain would never recover. We would not leave the hospital without a trach. We would not leave the hospital without a severely injured child on life support. Jude was gone.

It had been over an hour when the doctor, whose last name was ironically Justice, finally took a moment to speak to us. He knelt down next to us in the corner, his demeanor compassionate and kind. He spoke to us with a gentle tone and sympathetic, sad eyes.

"I need to tell you...we've been doing CPR for over an hour," he spoke softly, his gaze shifting between me and Jack.

Jack, his voice trembling with desperation, asked, "How much longer can we try?"

"Well, that's the question," he told us with a heavy sigh. "At a certain point, his brain has simply gone without oxygen for too long. I worry we are coming to that point."

He studied our expressions while I cried and Jack ran his fingers through his hair, desperate to think of a solution to a problem that had none. There was nothing else to do.

"I'll tell you what," the doctor said. "We will give him a few more rounds of medication and CPR."

It was a consolation gesture. There was no more

medication Jude could realistically take. There was no sign of life. They had been beating a dead body for over an hour.

After the last round of CPR, around 7:30 a.m., they called it. Jack asked if they could extubate him for us, and they kindly obliged. They removed his wires, and the medical staff quietly left the room, drawing the curtain behind them. Jude's tiny body was sprawled across the hospital bed.

He looked so small.

My knees hit the ground and the scream that had lived inside me all along was painfully extracted from my lungs, pouring onto the floor like vomit. Medical staff huddled in the hallway, and if it were not deemed inappropriate to cover their ears, they would have done so. The cries of a bereaved mother are of the most horrific sounds to hear. My sobs echoed from our room as tears streamed down my cheeks. Jack held our lifeless son in his arms.

Eventually, I lifted myself up and gazed through blurry eyes at the ungodly sight before me. Blood dripped from Jude's dark blue lips, his chest was purple and bruised, and his skin had turned a pale yellow color.

Jack laid Jude's body down and I crawled into bed next to him. It is nothing short of heartbreaking, the way your anguished mind seeks what it knows. I cuddled up to Jude as the nurses came to place a knitted blanket over us. I ran my fingers through his soft, blonde curls while singing his favorite lullabies, as if I could convince him to come back to me.

"See?" my shaky voice whispered to him. "Just like we used to. Remember?"

Memories flashed in my mind of taking naps with Jude when we had finally come home from the hospital, a dream of mine I'd held for months. I was so content to be able to cradle him in my arms and wrap him up in blankets, cuddling him close while we both rested our eyes. No tubes or wires or IVs came between us, no nurses took him away from me for dressing changes or blood draws. Our hearts finally beat together once again, and even though his breath sounds were always rattling through his congested lungs, my soul sang praises for each breath God gave him that did not need to be delivered by machines.

But here we were. It was silent. Even more silent than the ICU. There were no machine beeps, no breath sounds. There was no heartbeat like the one we heard on that first ultrasound in another lifetime, full of excitement and awe-struck wonder at our baby. Jack was kneeling by the hospital bed, holding onto Jude's hands and crying. Every now and then, Jack would move his hand, and against all common sense, my heart leapt out of my chest, for it wanted so badly to believe it was Jude moving. But Jude's body was only growing colder, decomposing in my very arms.

The PICU nurses were sobbing in the corner. Nurses who saw death everyday. Nurses who were not strangers to the bodies of dead children and the moans of their gutted parents. I thought of PICU staff as people who accepted the death of children as part of the job, but truthfully, they probably focused more on the business of saving children's lives. Jude was not one they coud save, and a dead child will make you sick to your stomach regardless of if it's in your job description or not. As they absorbed the devastating tragedy before them, I knew memories of Jude were showing up uninvited to their minds as well. All the smiles at morning rounds, bath times, and morning cuddles. All the milestones that cracked through stone made out of evidence-based skepticism. Thanksgiving day, the cutest bear costume you ever did see on Halloween, and taking family portraits of us on Christmas morning rang fresh in their memory. They were Jude's aunts and uncles. They helped raise him. Without their full knowledge or consent, Jude's light kissed their cheeks. They could not deny their rosy hue, for the warmth penetrated their tears and radiated off their skin when their fingertips brushed across the surface.

Without warning, Dr. M threw open the door and stumbled into the room. Someone had urgently alerted him about Jude's admission to the ER, and he immediately rushed to the hospital from his home. Upon seeing us, his body seemed to collapse against the door frame, his mouth agape in shock.

He was too late.

"No, no, no," he wailed to the sky, tears filling his eyes. Dr. M took a few tentative steps toward me, then crumbled to the floor, overcome with sorrow. I reached out, grabbing his hand as he cried.

"I can't be here," he confessed, his voice trembling with grief as he fled the room.

And what a normal, human response. Who among us does not instinctively turn on their heel and find the nearest exit when death enters? It's as intuitive as tracing your hands along a wall in a dark room in an attempt to find the light. It's a natural temptation to find a fresh coat of white paint to cover the bloody aftermath of tragedy splattered on the walls. But for those of us that are not mere observers, we know there is no choice for us. We know the stains have made their mark and have been set with fire. However much I wished I could escape the darkness, I knew that for the rest of my days, where I went, there it would meet me. I knew that part of me would be left right here on this hospital bed, cradling my dead son.

The coroner entered the room and told us he needed to photograph Jude's body. He also explained that, because Jude was just a child, they would later need to perform an autopsy. (Ultimately, they did not end up doing an autopsy because our doctors rallied against it, claiming there was more than enough medical history to show the death was of natural causes. They believed Jude had a mucus plug that he could not clear.) The coroner gently warned us that we were in our final moments with Jude. Jack, unable to face the permanence of the goodbye, asked if we could still see him one more time after the photographs. The coroner shifted uncomfortably as he kneeled on the floor next to us, the common position everyone seemed to take to do the delicate act of conversing with us. He said that yes, theoretically, we could see Jude one more time after that point — but it would need to be out of a body bag.

In those precious remaining moments, we chose to sing to Jude. Dr. M returned, joining us as we wept together, enveloping Jude in a cocoon of love and grief. Other nurses came down from the PICU to say their goodbyes. Our pastor, who had heard the news, arrived and was overcome with tears the moment he entered the room. He knelt with us, sobbing, praying, and singing over us. The hospital chaplain held our hands and asked if he could baptize Jude, to which we readily agreed. It was a sacred and intimate moment I will hold dear for the rest of my life, tenderly locked away in my heart, buried in that secret garden.

We whispered to Jude that he was such a strong baby, the strongest baby there ever was. We tucked him into the hospital bed and joked like we usually did that he was "snug as a bug in a rug." It was the same routine we followed every night for seven months, but this time, I knew I would not be returning to the hospital in the morning. I would not be rushing out the door to make it to morning rounds. I would not be greeted by his soft smiles and gentle morning stretches. I would likely live long enough to be forced to mourn him longer than I knew him. The fight was over. There was not "one more day" to get through.

I brushed his golden locks and proclaimed aloud

that the Lord was in this place, fulfilling the prophecy that Jude's life would be marked by praising the Lord at all times. With tears dripping onto the hospital sheets, I had to do the hardest thing I've ever had to do. I had to let go. His cold, limp hand fell from mine. I gave him one last look as I whispered my final "I love you" to my one and only firstborn child.

And with that, the flame of his life was extinguished. The last grain of sand fell between my fingers, never to be held again. Death was not playing games of amusement anymore. Death tore him from my embrace, shackled me to this monster called grief, turned out the light, and closed the door behind itself.

—

Life became a memory that drifted in the wind like dandelion seeds, a beautiful sight I once cherished in the innocence of childhood but now was not something I would deem worth chasing after. My body somehow managed to return to my front door after our pastor had driven us back to our apartment. I held a plastic bag of Jude's yellow onesie the paramedics had frantically cut through with scissors, leaving it a tattered mess of fabric. It was all that was left.

Everything in me went dark. I curled up on the couch, an empty bag of bones. Every part of me ached. The pressure in my head was throbbing. I noticed Jude's small white sock on the floor, triggering a memory I had months ago. It wasn't uncommon for me to find Jude's socks scattered in hidden places, under pillows and in between couch cushions. I remembered sharing a morbid thought aloud to Jack as I collected them:

"How terrible must it be for the people who lose their child, and then come back home and find these little baby socks tucked away under the pillow?" I said. Jack nodded but didn't want to entertain a thought that hit so close to home.

My eyes glared at my surroundings, and I hated everything I saw. I hated the furniture. I hated the microwave. I hated the floor and the walls. I hated the calendar marked with all of Jude's upcoming appointments. I hated everything that existed, I hated it purely because it existed, for it was without purpose. I did and said very little. Time had never moved so slowly as I continued to stare at the walls. I simultaneously wanted the time to pass while also dreading the encroaching darkness.

During that first week, I felt like a shadow of myself. Fortunately, our pastor's parents graciously offered their house, which they usually rented out, for us and our family to stay in. This change of physical space was tremendously needed because our apartment had become almost unbearable. Friends and family stayed with us as we dealt with logistical matters. We quickly rented a storage unit for Jude's belongings, packing them away because I couldn't bear to look at them any longer, yet I couldn't bring myself to part with them either. We organized Jude's memorial service at our church, opting for an intimate gathering but live-streaming it for those who wished to join remotely. We spent the days beforehand preparing videos, photo slideshows, speeches and music. Pouring our energy into his service and having a dedicated space to honor Jude were helpful.

The visits to the mortuary were difficult. The thought of Jude's lifeless body stowed in a refrigerator somewhere, separated from us, was deeply unsettling. The first time we visited to complete paperwork, we brought some clothes for Jude. The striped onesie I couldn't help but buy for him to wear on Easter when I passed the baby section in Target, a pair of jeans, and a pair of fuzzy socks Jack's mom had bought for him while we were still in the hospital.

The funeral chapel was exactly as you might expect,

adorned with floral-patterned couches and old mahogany furniture. The carpeted floor muffled each step we took. Everything was neat, almost too neat. I suppose it served as a distraction from the fact that they had dead bodies rotting in the other room. That tends to disturb people – the truth.

One of the funeral chapel workers asked us if we wanted to see Jude, knowing he was just down the hall. I hesitated before declining. They nodded politely before leading us to the director's office to fill out Jude's death certificate. When we gave him Jude's date of birth, he fell silent for a while.

"Oh, I'm...I'm very sorry," he muttered quietly. He asked us a few more questions before suggesting we view the urns in the other room. We chose cremation for Jude because I wanted to bring him back home. When we entered the room, the director struggled to find an urn that would be the right size for Jude. There weren't many options for us to look at. He clumsily explained that typically, urns were smaller for stillborn infants and neonates or slightly larger for children, but they didn't have many options for a one-year-old. Even in death, Jude didn't fit the mold. Jack and I hated all the urns, but we also just wanted to make a decision. We didn't particularly love urn shopping for our son. There was a blue one that had silver birds on it, which we deemed the least ugly, so we chose that one. When we got back to the director's office, he told us he would be waiving their service fees. We expressed our sincerest gratitude.

Once Jack and I got back in the car, we both mentioned how we wished one of the urns had a tree on it. Jude loved trees and stared at them often. In the mornings when he woke, he would stare in fascination at the tree outside our bedroom window for long periods of time. Sometimes, we could even observe his heart rate calming down on his pulse oximeter while he watched the leaves dance in the sunlight.

We hadn't even considered that there could be other options until it dawned on us that we could always look elsewhere to see if we could find an urn with a tree.

Online, I discovered a handcrafted brass sculpture of a tree that happened to rest atop a stainless steel box, resembling a piece of art more than a traditional urn. It was named "Tree of Life." We decided it was perfect for Jude and it was sent to our art gallery downtown after we purchased it. When we went to pick it up, the workers there all spoke so gently to us, as they knew the urn was for our one-year-old son. They had even included a signed card from them inside the box and didn't charge us for shipping, a gesture we found incredibly thoughtful.

On June 2, 2023, one year exactly from his initial cardiac arrest, Jude was cremated. It was emotional and heartbreaking, but I was so eager to have his body back home with us. One of the compassionate funeral chapel workers carefully placed the ashes in the urn for us, mentioning that it was one of the most beautifully crafted urns he had ever seen. He was a kind-hearted man who spent a considerable amount of time and effort to help us with anything we needed. He provided us with footprints and handprints of Jude, which needed to be done physically with ink. Typically, it's done digitally for adults, but only for their fingerprints. With very small babies, they can still use the digital scanner because their hands and feet fit on the screen that is usually used for an adult's finger. As always, Jude was atypical. He died at an inconvenient and unusual age, making the size of his hands too big for the scanner they could often use for babies who died shortly after birth.

The funeral chapel worker also cut us two locks of Jude's beautiful golden curls. We had called several times to make sure they had collected those before cremation, and he was never bothered by our pestering. I later learned that he and his wife had also experienced the loss of a child several years ago.

Jude now occupies the same spot where his bassinet once rested in the corner of our bedroom. Unlike some of his hospital rooms, I made sure he was positioned by the window so he could be washed in the light of the sun and gaze at the trees swaying in the wind. We got a small table with shelves underneath to be used as a memorial for him. It houses some of his favorite toys and books, as well as every letter anyone has ever written to us regarding Jude, from pregnancy to death. Next to his urn rests the electric candle our church gifted to us during our time at CHLA. I used to light it at the head of his crib each night before offering a prayer for him. I've wrapped the base of the urn in one of our favorite swaddles because I didn't like how the stainless steel felt perpetually cold. Even in death, a mother's instinct to care for her child does not die. Jude's memorial table holds a sacred and holy place in our lives, as does our grief. It's something to be displayed, preserved, and made beautiful. It echoes with a love that persists, resonating through the dark caverns of death, even if no one else is there to hear it.

I've come to realize that I'm privileged to comprehend a pain of this magnitude because our capacity for pain ultimately becomes our capacity for joy. As tragedy carves out craters of great depths in our hearts, they serve as reservoirs for potential treasure. The rains will come again, even in the driest wilderness, and the floodwaters will come pouring down into every empty space.

Psalm 84: 5-7 reads:
"Blessed are those whose strength is in you,
whose hearts are set on pilgrimage.
As they pass through the Valley of Baka,
they make it a place of springs;
the autumn rains also cover it with pools.

SOMETHING ABOUT SUFFERING

They go from strength to strength,
  till each appears before God in Zion."

    The Valley of Baka is commonly translated as the valley of weeping or the valley of tears. Though that pilgrimage will be full of despair, the journey toward God is not a typical one. Rather than becoming fatigued, this path leads you from strength to even more strength.

    Life's fullness is best experienced when we've developed the capacity for both heartache and delight. A grand perspective on life's gifts and trials will always seem like an unremarkable consolation prize when compared to the intense weight of suffering, but as deep as the chasms of sorrow travel — deeper still will the light follow. The dimmest star of all will not go unnoticed by you. Your vision will be refined to pick up every twinkling blessing tossed alongside the road by those who were too busy on their way to the sun.

11

All the Parts Suffer With It

"Carry each other's burdens, and in this way you will fulfill the law of Christ."
- Galatians 6:2 (NIV)

Here's the thing about grief — it makes people uncomfortable. I'll be the first to acknowledge that everyone navigates grief at their own pace and in their unique way. What might feel like healing balm to one grieving soul could feel entirely insensitive or aggravating to another. However, if there is someone in your life who is struggling, who is grieving, who is suffering — I would give this advice almost universally: show up, say something, be there.

All too often, the fear of saying the wrong thing paralyzes us. We justify our silence by convincing ourselves that there's truly nothing we can do to solve the problem. And, to be fair, that's accurate. I mean, realistically, what can you do? Cure someone's illness? Bring their loved one back to life? Persuade their family member to go to rehab?

The truth is, we are often powerless in the face of life's most challenging seasons. Whether it's in the weeks following a major life upheaval, like Jude's initial cardiac arrest when my world was destroyed, or in the weeks after his death, there was truly nothing anyone could say to make me feel even a little bit better. No words of encouragement, Bible verses, or inspirational quotes could console someone who feels like their life has been set ablaze. I believe that's part of the issue — we believe that if we can't provide a solution, then we have nothing to offer. Or perhaps, if we can't provide a solution, we simply don't want to offer anything at all. Lacking a solution should not concern you nearly as much as lacking compassion.

Compassion is often equated with kindness. We think of it as pitying someone and deciding to extend a helping hand. Deliverance is not an unimportant part of what compassion moves us to do, but it goes beyond that. If we delve into the word's etymology, "compassion" literally means to suffer with or to share in suffering.

I sometimes visualize it like this: you stumble upon someone who has fallen into a deep, dark pit. Concerned, you desperately search for a way to help them out. Sadly, there is no way; you lack the resources and the power to reach them, lift them out, or call for assistance. What do you do in this situation? Do you just offer a shrug and hope that they'll eventually find a way out? Maybe someone else will come along who can do more than you can.

This is often how it feels for someone who is struggling with immense tragedy or loss. Everyone stares at you from the top of the pit and tells you they're sorry. They share their best philisophical insights. They explain how or why you've fallen in. They might even drop off some flowers for you to look at. They show kindness. But, eventually, they need to get on their way. There's simply nothing they can do to pull you back up. You're too far down, buried in darkness, impossible to relate to. They tell you they'll come back around to check on you in a couple of days, and they do. Then they start saying to call if you need anything.

So, you might be thinking: okay, I see your point. But what more can I do?

Well...you jump.

That, my dear reader, is genuine compassion. It bears burdens. It suffers together. It leaps into the darkness alongside them. This is precisely what Jesus did for us when he experienced the human condition, one with humiliation, monotony, loneliness, frustration, abuse, and death. He suffered to the point of pleading with God for an alternative, and when his request was denied, he cried out that God had utterly forsaken him. He entered the empty pit. He willingly stepped into the shoes of every suffering human on Earth, those whose knees had hit the ground in anguish while they raised their voices to the heavens, believing God had abandoned them.

You need to jump out after them. You need to brave the waves with them. You need to get a taste of the weight they are carrying.

This is not going to be comfortable. In fact, it will be anything but. I would not be surprised if you didn't get a "thank you." However, it will be profoundly powerful. You will have provided the ministry of presence.

The day Jude died, our pastor presented us this gift of compassion. The second he walked through those emergency room doors, he was overwhelmed with tears. As a parent himself, he undoubtedly witnessed what could only be described as one of the most heart-wrenching tragedies to scar a human life. He could have kept his emotional distance. He could have shielded himself from fully grasping the depth of our pain because even imagining it would have been unbearable. But he knelt on the ground with us, sobbing as if it were his own son, his own tragedy.

He embodied Jesus when he saw that his friend Lazarus had died. Jesus knew death was nothing to be feared, and he even knew that he would bring Lazarus back, but he didn't preach that to anyone. Jesus himself did not quote scripture or offer solutions or explanation in such a time. Instead, he knelt over Lazarus' dead body and wept. He shared in their loss and grieved the heartbreaking truth that humanity will succumb to death. The Lord is gracious and *compassionate.*

Jesus not only modeled how to give compassion, but how one depends upon it. In the garden of Gethsemane, Jesus tells his followers he is "overwhelmed with sorrow to the point of death." He confesses his need for them. He pleads with them to stay.

They don't.

When our pastor drove us home, he came into our living room and sat on the floor. I didn't offer him water or pull out a chair or engage in small talk. I didn't speak to him at all. I didn't have the capacity to provide him one bit of comfort. I simply sat on the couch, deeply traumatized and sick to my stomach. Birthday decorations and toys were scattered around the floor, and they might as well have been bloodstains. Entryway rugs were strewn about to allow the paramedics to easily transport Jude outside. Jude's ventilator and medical cart loomed ominously in our bedroom. We couldn't touch anything because we had to wait for the police to arrive and take photographs, as if it were a crime scene. Our lives had become the dark, eerie house on the side of the road, its windows echoing with screams of agony that you'd like to cautiously retreat from — but our pastor chose to enter through the front door and meet whatever darkness had enveloped us. In silence, on a Tuesday morning, on our living room floor, with nothing to offer — there he sat.

The next morning, another friend of mine who had heard what happened texted me, asking if she could come over. I said yes. I was in bed when I heard her at the door, and I got up to let her in. I can't imagine I was a great sight to behold. She was a new, first-time mother herself, and she came in with several Starbucks bags holding various breakfast foods. She never asked me what I wanted, or what kind of food sounded good, or if I had eaten yet. She simply walked in, placed the bags on the counter, and told me that she had picked up a few different things that I could choose to eat or not, but there they were. She sat on the couch right next to me while I sobbed.

"I'm in so much pain," I wailed.

Her eyes welled with tears and she nodded, wrapping her arm around me. She told me how sorry she was, held me while I cried, and allowed her heart to break. When she had to leave, she admitted to me that she would be crying the whole way home. She allowed her life to be interrupted with an overwhelming suffering that she knew she could walk away from, and I could not. So she carried it for a small while.

One of my more endearing memories of a compassionate friend was the week after Jude died. I hadn't spent much time at my apartment, but I happened to visit one afternoon with some friends and family to drop off Jude's urn, which we had just purchased, and gather a few belongings. While we were all sitting on my living room floor, there was a knock at the door, and it was one of my friends who had unexpectedly shown up. She was holding a pack of La Croix.

"Hi," she said hesitantly. "I just wanted to come by and see you and...I brought this."

She awkwardly held out the La Croix to me and I grabbed it from her with a smile. She came in and sat with us — me and a group of people she had never met. We didn't do much, just talked about plans for Jude's funeral and things I still had to get done around the apartment. I showed her Jude's urn and a few other people knocked on my door to pay me a visit or drop off some flowers. I mentioned that it was funny she came at that time because it was one of the very small windows I actually happened to be in my apartment. She told me she was just hanging around at home and thought to come see me.

What I loved most about her visit was that silly little pack of La Croix. The fact that she had the idea to come see me and, before coming, glanced around her apartment to see if there was anything she could bring so she wouldn't arrive empty-handed was heartwarming. She could have easily talked herself out of coming by thinking that she hadn't been invited or perhaps she should send a text first or that it felt awkward to drop by with just a pack of La Croix. So what? She grabbed the thing closest to her that was available and came by. La Croix was not going to solve my problems, but she didn't allow the lack of a solution to be the reason she had a lack of compassion. She didn't have a beautifully arranged bouquet of flowers, a sympathy card, a list of my favorite comfort foods she could provide, or probably any idea of what she would even say to me. She picked up a case of sparkling water in her fridge because it was what she had to offer. She showed up at my door with no particular thing to say because it was what she could think of to do. She didn't get lost in a sea of thought about herself or if she was bringing the best thing or saying the right thing or offering the right solution. She just showed up at my doorstep because I was broken-hearted and brought a beverage because I'm a human being who needs to drink water. It's really that simple.

No, you can't solve everyone's problems. You might not know their dietary preferences, you might not look your best, you might not have the words to say, you might not be comfortable. So what if you're uncomfortable? They're in agony. And even people in agony still need to eat. They still need their dishes cleaned. They still need their laundry washed. They still need their kids looked after. They still need their bills paid. They still need someone who can come alongside them and help bear the burden, even if they don't have the power to take it away completely. Obviously, there is no love language that blots out pain, but I cannot tell you the healing power of every last person who sent a card, showed up at my front door, dropped off flowers, or simply came to sit with me. It doesn't make the grief stop, but it demonstrates that they were willing for their world to stop, even for a moment, in acknowledgment that mine had violently halted. I can't imagine how worse the grief would have been if everyone who decided to do anything, did nothing at all, simply because they figured it wouldn't help.

Jack had a friend who called him the day Jude died just to tell him how sorry he was. I don't even think much else was said, but he stayed on the line for a while — just there. I'm sure that was anything but comfortable. I can't imagine he felt adequately prepared on what to say. What he did know is that he couldn't go to sleep that night without calling, without lowering himself into the pit, even for a moment. Even just to say, "I know that you're in pain. I'm so sorry. I'm here. I'm going to sit right here next to you."

Studies have shown that profanity decreases physical pain. If someone repeats a swear word while their hand is submerged in ice water, they can withstand the pain longer than if they were not to swear at all.

There are two favorite responses I have witnessed to my grief: tears and profanity. These two things can only come from someone who has done the work of plunging their hand into the ice water. It shows me they are feeling something. They are trying to understand.

Out of all the comments on our public announcement that Jude had passed away, among all the "thoughts and prayers" and "I'm sorry for your loss" this is the one that weirdly brought me the most comfort: "This doesn't feel fair.

This feels fucked up." If that's not the thought that crosses your mind when you imagine a dead child being stowed away in a refrigerator like the spinach you bought to make yourself feel better but know you're going to let wilt as you carry on with life, then you aren't trying very hard.

After Jude died it felt like my heart was ripped outside of my chest and on display for everyone to see. It is our responsibility as decent human beings to handle that with care. In a vulnerable state like that, someone needs a soft place to land, and even the most well-intentioned words can feel as comforting as a pumice stone. Carelessness or cruel dismissal can make them throw the nearest blanket over their bleeding heart in an embarrassed attempt to hide their mess, their pain, their soul. They will retreat back into themselves, trapped in a darkness they don't believe will ever end. Show them that their tragedy is safe with you. Don't try to silence it — let grief make a mess on your newly purchased white rug. Be careful. Be present. Be compassionate.

None of us take a course on this. My hope is that all of us can extend grace to one another. I don't know how to lose my son any more than you know how to talk to someone who lost their son. But I can tell you, the most hurtful things were never the words that were said, but the words that were not said. The ones who never called, who never wrote, who never knocked. The ones who saw me in the pit and walked by because they deemed it beyond their capacity. Most people don't want to eat, but what they want even less is to have to think about what to eat. Just drop something off and go on your way. They don't have to eat it, but it will mean the world that you took at least one decision off their plate. If you're too nervous to see them in person, write a card. I can't tell you how deeply I still treasure every handwritten card. I saved each one like precious gemstones. Some people don't want to talk about their grief, but most do. Ask questions. The loss of a child is commonly considered an "unimaginable" tragedy for most to comprehend. Grief expert and bereaved parent David Kessler has expressed his discomfort with that perspective, saying, "...but you don't have to imagine. I'm right here in front of you. It's happening to me right now. *Talk* to me."

All of these people in my life saw a completely different side of my grief journey. One I didn't even make eye contact with, one I sobbed my heart out to, and one I talked to in a relatively normal fashion. You never can fully prepare for jumping into the pit. You don't know what you'll find once you hit the ground. The important thing is, you jumped.

That's what they will remember. That's all any of us will remember. A warm hand placed on ours.

12

When You Must Bury

"I will not cause pain without allowing something new to be born, says the Lord."
- Isaiah 66:9 (NCV)

The night after Jude died was the single worst night of my life. I tried to close my eyes but couldn't physically hold still. I thrashed and squirmed around in bed, attempting to overcome the insatiable need I had to crawl out of my own skin. It was as if I were having withdrawal symptoms from losing him the way an addict would from losing a drug. I sobbed and moaned as the ache only grew, and images of him dying in my arms haunted me relentlessly. The memories came back like a swinging baseball bat each time, beating me into the ground. I fell onto the carpet as the bat continued to rail into my ribs, my stomach, my skull. Again and again. Bones were splitting and organs were punctured. I spit the blood out of my mouth and wondered how my broken body was still alive, how it could possibly withstand it.

Around 3 a.m., you would have followed the trail of bubbling red blood out of my bedroom, across the hall, into Jude's room. There, I collapsed on the floor, screaming into a pillow while the weight of his death suffocated me.

When you imagine what receiving a blessing might look like, I'm sure this disturbing image of a 26-year-old crying on the floor of her dead son's Peter Rabbit-themed bedroom is not exactly what comes to mind. But in that raw, bloody, heart-wrenching moment, God tells me I was blessed.

"Blessed are those who mourn, for they shall be comforted." - Matthew 5:4

God blesses the broken. God comforts those who feel cursed. But I felt utterly alone. I did not feel comforted. I did not feel blessed. I did not feel like God was near. I did not feel at peace with the idea that Jude was in heaven with Jesus. That idea didn't even ring true for me because it didn't feel like Jude was in heaven; it felt like Jude was a decomposing body in funeral chapel down the street.

The word bereavement means to be robbed of or ripped away from. It has been described as losing a limb from your body, not an amputation cleanly done through surgical means or medical tools, but to literally be torn off. A scene so awful to witness you wouldn't even be able to stand the sound of it, let alone the sight.

What do we do about Jesus' words that it is the poor, the hungry, the grieving who are blessed? What do we do about the fact that all but one of Jesus' apostles were brutally martyred? What do we do about God's will for Jesus being one of ridicule, loneliness, poverty, and torture? What do we do about the life of Job, a blameless man who had his wealth, his health, and all of his children taken from him? What do we do about childhood cancer? What do we do about the parents who must watch their child struggle with addiction? What do we do about innocent civilians brutally raped and murdered in war crimes? What do we do about the millions that will die of diseases we have a cure for? What do we do about the mother who gives birth to a stillborn infant, where death precedes life?

We cling to the Holy Spirit who dwells in the dark. Yes, God is with you when you marry, but he is especially with you when you bury. He is with you on the surface but he is especially with you in the depths. He is with you, dear reader, in your comfortable home, but he is especially within the refugee camps and violent war zones. God hears us all, but his ear is inclined to the cries of the oppressed.

Death can and will devastate absolutely everything — except for God's kingdom. It's not that God is necessarily closer, but that we have the ability to experience him deeper when the painful process of stripping away false hopes has been done. We not only are exposed to our own dependency on God, but our dependency on each other. It becomes evident that we need the people in our lives to not remain mere observers but to act as a search and rescue team, prepared to jump out after us. We need the various gifts that others can offer, whether it's financial expertise, uplifting support, or the willingness to clean a messy kitchen.

The God of the Bible is one who allows suffering to pass. While this perspective might differ from what you commonly heard in Sunday School, I don't know how one could conclude otherwise. Suffering is one of his primary means of sanctification — and I know you don't feel sanctified, you feel broken. But who says brokenness can't be holy? Pain serves as a tool through which he uses the enemy's own devices against him, trialing us by fire and forging precious gemstones through a metamorphism of sorts. In the words of J. R. R. Tolkien, what punishments of God are not gifts?

So, don't merely attempt to prepare for the darkness, for there is no such way to prepare for it. Instead, anticipate it, dear reader, and understand that it lies beyond your control. Remind yourself that you are doing the best you can. Lightning doesn't exclusively strike metal rods and death shows no discrimination. Poverty can befall the well-prepared and depression can ensnare even the most devoted disciple. Tragedies will find us, our families and our friends.

Our cries fall short of the unrelenting storm clouds.

Don't be afraid to challenge God to a wrestling match. A prayer of lament is still a prayer. You can make room. You can make room for the pain and the fear and the unmet desires. You can confide in him with your traumas, your grief, and your weary, exhausted soul. Recognizing that he is God and you are not, even if born out of frustration and anger, is an act of reverence.

That night, while I knelt in despair, I did not have hope. I pleaded that God would end my life. I did not have faith. I did not want to live another day. And yet, God reminds us of something greater, something transcending all anguish — love. God's love poured down on me, his blessings whispered over me, his Spirit drew near to me, whether I felt them or not. In the darkest abyss where hope's voice falters across the distance and faith's footing vanishes beneath the waves, where darkness envelops us, God's love is deeper still.

"For I am convinced that neither death nor life, neither angels nor demons, neither the present nor the future, nor any powers, neither height nor depth, nor anything else in all creation, will be able to separate us from the love of God that is in Christ Jesus our Lord."
- Romans 8:38-39.

One of the most powerful things I've come to appreciate is God's unwavering, relentless love. If I'm honest with myself, I do not possess the same all-consuming, all-pursuing love for God in my heart. The temptations of this world often distract me, and as a human, I'm prone to crafting idols from the very materials intended for me as gifts. If following God means persecution, suffering, and ultimately death — I choose not to follow God. I choose not to follow him every time.

Following God is a narrow, tumultuous path. It is riddled with the death of the innocent and a life of humility and service to the poor. It commands us to take the high road without guarantee of acknowledgment and encourages a lowly spirit that gives more than it takes. Are you that humble, selfless soul? Because I am not. In a thousand lifetimes, I don't know that I could ever conjure up the ability to consistently choose whichever path that led me to God, regardless of the sacrificial requirements. My nature leans towards self-preservation. If I were faced with two paths, one with Jude but without God, or one without Jude but with God, I fear I wouldn't choose God. I'm afraid I do not possess that strength.

Oh, but he chooses me.

He chooses me regardless of whether I choose him. Like a stubborn, tantrum-throwing child fixated on the allures of this world, I resist him kicking and screaming even as he tenderly guides me to bed. He values my character over my comfort, and despite my obstinate selfishness, he welcomes me into his kingdom. He teaches me how to hold every part of this life loosely, like sand flowing through my fingers. He shows me how to see every ray of light as a gift given, not an entitlement deserved. He reminds me that I'm not the main character in humanity's narrative. He is the parent assuring me I needn't throw a fit over placing my most precious toy on the high shelf in the closet overnight, for it will be waiting for me in the morning. Nothing is ever lost that he cannot restore.

In our lowest points, I couldn't help but feel as though God were tormenting me with worst-case scenarios. Looking back, I realize it was my own greed, demanding the return of something that was, in reality, a gift to begin with. I understand now that there exists no scenario in which my child dies that would ever feel sufficient. There are no limits to the "if onlys" and "what ifs" that convince us things could somehow be better. Grief is heavy enough as it is, you do not need to add to its measure. There's no way you could have known. There's no way you could have changed the outcome. The grieving mind is never satisfied.

When Jack and I prayed for Jude that night of his first cardiac arrest on June 2, God allowed him to be revived. He gave us almost exactly 365 days with Jude on this Earth. Despite the severity of the event, against all odds, Jude became alert and interactive with his environment. He was social, he smiled, he made relationships with us. He communicated to us when he was happy or sad, relieving me of the constant uncertainty about his inner world. God gave us hope for Jude. He graced us with the gift of replacing some of our most painful memories with outings to the beach, walks in the park, reading Jude's favorite books, celebrating unlikely yet remarkable milestones, and cherishing precious moments cuddled together in bed. He allowed us to gather our friends and family to celebrate Jude's life on his first birthday, letting those who had prayed for him witness the impact of their prayers. All this time, I had been fighting for Jude to go home, and now he is. God granted us more time with a soul always destined to return home to *him*, and for that, I am profoundly grateful.

He reminds me that I am like someone standing on the opposite side of a tapestry, surrounded by loose threads, unable to see the masterpiece. In my pursuit of gratitude, he grants me the strength to embrace the truth that the joys and sorrows of our existence are inextricably woven. He does not chastise me when I lament this life and lose all faith; instead, he remains by my side until the cries of my soul quiet long enough to hear that sweet song of hope still echoing on the horizon.

There is something about this suffering I cannot yet see. The storm will pass as surely as it will come. He is composing a victory over sin and death. He assures me the

pain won't be wasted.
He will do a new thing.
He will make it count.

To Jude, From Mom

My love,

Your life brought me the deepest joy I've ever known, and its loss was the deepest pain I'd ever experienced. Though the grief is heavy, I hold a weighty gratitude for the privilege of knowing you, of loving you, and caring for you — I would have gladly done so for the rest of my days.

You had every reason to be unhappy, yet you beamed at everyone who entered your presence. Even when they came to perform painful procedures, you forgave quickly and were happy to see them return. You loved to be included in everything, rolling across the living room floor and into the kitchen to eavesdrop on our conversations. You woke up each morning with a smile, as if you didn't expect another day, as if you knew you were on borrowed time. How blessed we were to have had that time together.

You were joyful, mischevious, resilient, miraculous, curious, intelligent, playful, long-suffering, innocent, and so important. I would relive every storm of this life if it meant I could be the mom of such a life for another 365 days. I would endure endless days in hospitals, surviving on minimal sleep and cafeteria food if it meant I could hold you in my arms once more. I now view life through a veil of sadness, but I hold faith that God will restore. Your life held so much purpose.

I think of you every day, my sunshine. I imagine God must have quite a shelf to store all the bottles of my tears he has collected.

I hope you are finally experiencing the joy of eating, with mango juice dribbling down your chin. I hope your body moves freely, and you no longer struggle to play with your favorite toys or flip the pages of your dearest books. I hope you can take a nice, deep breath. I trust they are taking good care of you there.

There was a reverend named Brad who baptized you shortly after your time with us had ended. He also attended your funeral and shared many wise words with us about where our hope lies. I still have an underlying suspicion that he was somewhat of an angel. I want to share with you the speech he gave at your baptism:

"When the Lord talks about baptism, he taught us to do that in the context of family and community. We never know the time, we never know the reasons why, but we do know that the Lord is here and present. He is with Jude and he's with you and he's with each of us. There are hundreds of promises of the Lord being here with us, and as a minister of the gospel of Jesus Christ, it is my honor to join together our hearts and our souls and our minds in acknowledging Jude as God's precious child. Jude, I baptize you in the name of the Father, the Son and the Holy Spirit. Rest, grace and peace to you. May the Lord bless you and keep you, may the Lord make his face shine upon you, may the Lord lift his countenance upon you and give you peace – now and forevermore.

Taylor and Jack, thank you for being so faithful to Jude. Thank you for the ways in which you loved him and will always love him. He will always, always be in your heart. Never separated – just a season. And you will, in the morning, be together again. For a time separated, but forever and ever together. I pray these things in the Father, in the Son, and in the Holy Spirit. In Jesus' holy name, amen."

His words remind me of a thought-provoking letter Einstein once wrote. He believed that every point in the past and every point in the future is just as real as the present time we exist in right now. When Einstein's dear friend passed away, he penned a letter to the friend's wife, expressing his perspective on life and death. In his letter, he conveyed that time resembles a landscape with past, present, and future all connected as one. He assured her that her late husband was merely beyond the next hill. Though she couldn't see him at that moment, he existed just as profoundly as ever — just over that hill. Her view was simply obstructed in the part of the landscape where she resided. He closed his handwritten letter to her with this:

"Now he has again preceded me a little in parting from this strange world. This has no importance. For people like us who believe in physics, the separation between past, present and future has only the importance of an admittedly tenacious illusion."

And so, I will persist in returning to that west-facing window, where I gaze at the dark horizon. Though we are separated momentarily, as a great mind once said, this is of no importance. For I know the sun will rise, and I shall see you again in the morning.

All my love,
Mom

To Jude, From Dad

It's hard to believe now, but there was once a time before I met you. Momma and I fell in love, got married, and began to dream about you. When I first felt you move, I knew I was in trouble because I only wanted to discover new ways to get you to kick again. You were the most active baby when you were in your Momma. Once, when your Momma rubbed ice on her belly, we watched through her belly as your little hand tracked the ice cube wherever it went. We were so excited about you. The moment you entered the world, the entire room fell away, and while I was all but consumed by awe and emotion, I couldn't take my eyes off of you. Although you were only 8 pounds, 2 ounces, there was a heaviness about you, and I realized I would never be the same as the person who didn't know you.

At first, I was afraid to touch or hold you; you were so small, so soft, so trusting. Even at the time, I knew your first week was one of the greatest of my life, and I longed for time to standstill. It was incredible to watch how quickly Momma and you were in love, and it was humbling to know how much I loved you both.

When your heart stopped, I was so scared. But you were strong, so much stronger than I have ever been. For weeks, I stood right over your bed, stepping away for a few hours to sleep but never letting you leave my sight or thoughts. I prayed for you to do *anything*. When I heard other children cry, I could only think that I would give anything to hear you cry, not because I could even stomach the thought of you in pain, but because it would be a sign you were alive. I felt as if I had to breathe for you, that it was my job to keep you alive, but in reality, I could never do what you did. Of all the people I have met, nobody was stronger than you, nobody was tougher than you, and nobody was more impressive. Each new thing you did felt like a miracle: when you first reacted to the doctors, looked at me, or made a noise. Everything you did was beyond what we could expect, what anyone thought was possible. I waited on your every noise, every movement, and every emotion as if there was nothing else in the world more important than what you did and who you were. I don't think I ever stopped being enthralled by even the smallest things you did.

When you began to show the doctors signs of consciousness, I told them I was the luckiest person in the world. When you first cried, I cried with gratitude. The nurses and doctors were amazed when you began to track with your eyes, and I couldn't take *my* eyes off of you. The first time you smiled at Momma, I knew there was nothing in the world that could be better.

Your Momma was there for you through everything. Once she was allowed to hold you, there wasn't a day in which most of your hours weren't in her arms. On days you were in pain and cried from seven in the morning until they gave you pain meds at nine at night, on days when you were sick and tired and just wanted to cuddle, or on days when

165

you were happy and playful and wanted to turn the pages on every book in your library, your Momma held you in her arms and rarely put you down. She gave you all she could and never tired but only wanted to give you more of herself. No person I have met has ever demonstrated the Christ-like love of giving all of oneself the way she so freely gave her everything to you, her little peanut.

When you finally came home, I felt like my cup overflowed with blessings so undeserved. When I talked to anyone, I couldn't help but tell them that you were rolling, sitting, holding toys, or beginning to put food to your mouth and swallow. I was utterly proud of everything you did; regardless of how small, it felt larger than the world. You were just so impressive to me. But if you never did anything else, I would still have loved you dearly and been so proud of you, my little bud. Even if you never walked, talked, ate by mouth, or anything else, you would have been my son and my most valuable treasure. I have about 6,000 photos of you, and my photo album is more valuable than my bank account. If I was nothing else, I was entirely proud and amazed by you, my baby boy.

It was the morning after your birthday when you died. I tried to save you; I tried with all that I knew how to do, but I couldn't do it. It happened so quickly; one moment, you were looking at me with your soul behind those blue eyes, and then you just weren't. It didn't seem like you hurt.

After you died in the ER, we held you for hours before we had to say goodbye, although it wasn't enough, and I knew it could never be enough. I hope you weren't scared, little one.

We kissed your cheeks, Momma held you in her arms, and I held your hand like we did at home. I sang your songs, prayed thanks for your life, and did my best to say the things that I wanted to say during the last time I would ever get to see your beautiful face — the closest thing to perfection in a world that is not. I wasn't ready to say goodbye to you, my love, although I don't know if I ever would've been. I'm sorry that I wasn't able to protect you.

You loved music, my dear. Even when your life brought you pain, or you just couldn't sleep, I would sing, and peace would rush across your face. I sang "Amazing Grace" to you almost every day, before bed or a nap, and you listened to every note, regardless of how poorly I sang it. You thought "I'm a Little Teapot" was hilarious; you would just crack up every time I made you into the teapot. Nothing would make you beam and smile as joyfully as when Momma sang "You are My Sunshine." Although, I think you thought the alphabet song was the most interesting. I would sign the letters to you and sing, and even if you were getting poked by needles, you would fixate on my hands. Oh, how much you loved hands: watching hands, playing with hands, having your hands caressed when you were uncomfortable. You loved to hold my hand, with your little fist wrapped tightly around my finger. I loved to hold your hand, too, my child.

You were just the sweetest boy. You were simply born like that. While you experienced a lot of hurt in the hospital, by the time you made it home, you rarely cried without becoming completely happy again just by being picked up into our arms. You just wanted to be held, like you knew every moment with us could be your last, and you didn't want us to waste any of it.

Momma and I couldn't stop saying that you were the happiest baby. We thought it was hilarious to watch you roll around the living room to get to some toy or into the kitchen to say, "Hey there!" You thought it was funny to see us from afar. If we made eye contact across the room, and I said, "Hey baby!" you would giggle and laugh like it was the funniest thing you had ever seen. We did that for hours like it was our inside joke. I loved to see you laugh, especially when I couldn't figure out why you found something so funny. But I think my life's favorite memories are the ones where you laugh at the silly games you played with Momma. You were so happy and funny, my little sweet bean.

There was so much I still wanted to do with you. Momma and I hoped to take you around the world and show you all the places that we loved to go. We hoped you would have friends, those who loved you dearly, and maybe even someone you would love enough to marry. I wish I could've taught you how to play the music you loved so much or taken you to your first day of school. I know you would have grown to be an incredible man and a loving human being. I am not ready to say goodbye to you yet, my little bear. I was prepared to give you anything and wanted to show you everything.

You loved trees. You didn't get to see many for the first seven months of your life, but when you came home, you loved to look at them. You would wake up in the morning, sit up, and stare at the trees outside our window while I tried to get thirty minutes more sleep. You thought they were beautiful, and they brought you peace.

We decided to put your ashes into a sculpture of a tree, and I think that you would have liked that. I hope you feel peace now, and while we cannot hold you again in this world, I know you are not crying, and we will be with you again. I believe God desires for the brokenness, chaos, and death of this world to end, replaced with love like two in a garden by the Tree of Life. I hope your urn is a testament to that faith and our hope that we will hold you again with no more tears, no more sickness, and unending love.

My everything longs to hold you again and spot your two little top teeth when I make you laugh. You are so beautiful to me, my son, and I am so proud of all that you are. You are stronger, kinder, more loving, and better than I ever could be. I will miss our bath times, after which you would roll away from me so I wouldn't dress you. I will miss kissing your head at night, our morning mirror games, and taking you on afternoon walks. I will miss getting to know you, watching you grow up, and falling in love with you more. I will love you forever and miss you for the rest of my life.

Until I hold you again,
Dad

"and provide for those who grieve in Zion — to bestow on them a crown of beauty instead of ashes, the oil of joy instead of mourning, and a garment of praise instead of a spirit of despair. They will be called oaks of righteousness, a planting of the Lord for the display of his splendor."

- Isaiah 61:3 (NIV)

Did this book help you in some way? If so, I'd love to hear about it. Please leave a review on Amazon. Honest reviews help readers find the right book for their needs.

Thank you for reading Jude's story.

Taylor Keefer was raised in a log cabin in the forests of northwestern Montana, where she discovered her passion for storytelling at a young age. Today, she and her husband live a simple life on the sunny central coast of California, where they never have to choose between the mountains or the sea.

Embracing the beauty of the outdoors, they find solace in their faith, and together, they cherish the memory of their beloved son, Jude, who is in heaven. Taylor's writing reflects her profound experiences in navigating grief, faith, and the remarkable endurance of the human spirit.

taylorelizabethkeefer.com
Instagram: @taylorkeefer_
Youtube: @taylorkeefer1068

Made in the USA
Middletown, DE
07 November 2023

42137804R00109